Y0-DJN-953

ACCEPTED

ACCEPTED

BY

STUART KAHAN

ALLWORTH PRESS, NEW YORK

© 1992 by Stuart Kahan

All rights reserved. Copyright under Berne Copyright Convention, Universal Copyright Convention, and Pan American Copyright Convention. No part of this book may be reproduced, stored in a retrieval system, or transmitted in any form, or by any means, electronic, mechanical, photocopying, recording or otherwise, without prior written permission of the publisher.

Published by Allworth Press, an imprint of Allworth Communications, Inc., 10 East 23rd Street, New York, NY 10010.

Distributor to the trade in the United States: Consortium Book Sales & Distribution, Inc., 287 East Sixth Street, Suite 365, Saint Paul, MN 55101.

Book design by Douglas Design Associates, New York, NY.

Library of Congress Catalog Card Number: 92-71566

ISBN: 1-880559-01-3

Cover photograph courtesy of Lynchburg College.

TABLE OF CONTENTS

SOCIAL SCIENCE & HISTORY DIVISION

R00926 06703

INTRODUCTION

- "The government has cut educational costs drastically and there's no money available for college."
- "There is no such thing as financial need unless you are destitute."
- "It doesn't pay to apply to the good schools. Their costs are sky high."

You believe any of this? Well, a recent poll for the Council for the Advancement and Support of Education showed that 87% of the people in the U.S. think college is out of reach for most of us.

That's what they *think*. But here are the real facts:

- "There's more money than ever available for college today."
- "The government has actually increased aid to education."
- "You don't have to be destitute to get financial aid."
- "You can apply to and afford even the best private schools."

In short, money *does* exist.

Try these numbers on for size. Last year alone, there was some $26 billion—that's with a B—available in financial aid for college. This is an increase over the $21 billion in 1990. For next year, the projection is to top the $28 billion mark.

Know what the problem is? Many people never tap into this huge reservoir of money simply because they don't know how to do it. Practically every college has a list of grants and scholarships that lay dormant from year to year because no one ever looks for the money. Incredible, but true!

And what about the myth that says a family income has to be at the poverty level in order to be able to receive financial aid? Look at Antioch College, in Yellow Springs, Ohio, as one example of many. Antioch says that their commitment is to meet 100% of each student's financial needs. And they back this up. Last year, Antioch's student budget, or direct costs, for attending the school was $16,450. A family of five, with two in college, and $78,325 in assets and adjusted gross income (certainly *not* at the poverty level) received a financial aid package totaling $13,575.

Exception to the rule? Not in the least. Susquehanna University in Selinsgrove, Pennsylvania, maintains that it is committed to offering both a high-quality private education and the financial aid necessary to give the student an educational choice. And, they back this up by showing that for the class of 1994, some 415 students out of 500 were awarded financial aid at an average of $10,172 toward a tuition/fees total of $13,120.

And, in New York State, some 75% of full-time undergraduate students attending independent colleges receive help. That represents more than $750 million in aid in one state alone.

Still believe the myths?

So, push aside those naysayers and take a look at what's *really* going on. The first thing to do is *not* to listen to the voices of doom who claim there is nothing around. You'd be surprised at what may be waiting for you just beneath the surface.

Why This Book Was Written

When it comes to finding the right college, getting into it and paying for it, this is the real book for the 90s. It is a first. I know, you've heard that claim before; however, for once, it's true. There has been no book like this on the market and if you have a high school senior being readied for college, or you are that senior, then you will quickly see that there is a crying need for the information contained within these pages.

This book was written because I heard similar complaints from both parents and students alike. From the high school senior: "I want to go to college but I'm not sure which one would be the best for me. Do I want to stay home? Kerry is going to commute. She's my girl friend. Or, do I want to go away? Michael is going out of town. He's my boy friend. But, I'm not sure I want to go as far as he is. Then again, I'm not sure what I want to take up anyway. I wish I had more knowledge."

From the parent: "I know she's not a great student but I would like to see her in a good school. When we do we have to apply? Do we need to apply to more than one? How do we improve the chances of getting her in? And, what about the costs? We can afford a state school but not a private one. Is there financial aid available at all schools and if so, how do we go about getting some?"

To say that these queries only scratch the surface would be an understatement. The questions both parents and students ask are mind-boggling. For example, try these on for size:

1) How do I find the better schools?

2) What are they anyway?

3) How do I evaluate which is the best one for me, for my purposes? Aren't there criteria?

4) What's the secret of getting into such a school?

5) Will a low SAT score or grade point average really knock out the better schools?

6) What are the deadlines for the application forms? When's the best time to submit same?

7) How do I coordinate the SAT scores, the application forms and other documentation?

8) What about that crazy financial aid form? How do I figure it out? Besides, is there really money out there?

9) Are there scholarships available for non-athletes?

10 Do I need any interviews?

This book is designed to help every student and every parent in selecting, getting into and paying for the right college. To be sure, there are many books on the library shelves about colleges, plus a number on financial aid, but there is nothing around to take you by the hand and lead you step-by-step through the entire process. Also, there is no book backed by the experience, care and proven results as this one. In effect, this book was written for myself. It's the end result of my own accomplishments as a parent of five children in getting four of my kids (the fifth one comes up this year) into good colleges without having to pay through the nose for the privilege.

Actually, this is the kind of book I wish I had when faced with sending the first of my brood to school. Thus, the procedures you will read here represent the outcome of my success. Immodestly, it has become the format that a number of high-ranking educators in New York State, plus various guidance counselors and college administrators have held up as the prototype.

At first, many of these learned people looked down at what I considered innovative procedures. Some told me at the beginning I would be doomed to failure. But that has changed dramatically. These same people have now seen what can be accomplished with imagination, paying homage to detail and the ability to say, "It can be done."

How This Book Was Written

The idea behind all of this surfaced with my oldest son. Here's what happened.

He was in his last month of the junior year at high school. He wanted to go to college. He was talking about being a biology major, perhaps enrolling in a pre-medicine program. His grades were good, a 3.5 average although his SAT scores were not commensurate, only 980. However, he had a lot of other things going for him. He was quarterback of the football team, a top wrestler and active in student government. A number of colleges, in fact, already expressed interest in him. This was especially gratifying to me, but from my own experience I also knew the ins and outs of the student-athlete. Although my son was good, he was not a superstar and besides, he didn't want a big school. Therefore, he seemed to be talking about what is known as Division III...and they don't give athletic scholarships.

At this point, you should know something about me. I have an inordinate interest in colleges. Actually, it would be better to say that I am in love with them. If I am driving and there's a sign pointing to a college, I'll take the detour no matter how many miles it takes me away from my planned destination. Show me ivy-covered walls and I melt. Maybe it's because I had the best four years of my life during college or maybe it's because I traveled to many other campuses to see former high school classmates. Who knows? But, I have a great deal of knowledge when it comes to colleges. I know that the view from Michie Stadium at the U.S. Military Academy at West Point offers the most dramatic and beautiful setting of any college in the country, that the state of Pennsylvania is recognized as having a preponderance of the nation's top liberal arts colleges and that the University of California at Berkeley consistently receives high academic honors in polls of educators, even beating out the famed Harvard for first place.

So, universities to me are analogous to eating potato chips. I can't stop after one.

With this in mind, I now had the opportunity, the first since my own college days some twenty-five years ago, to pour over catalogues again and construct visits to campuses. I had a burst of energy that sustained me all summer long and an interest that became obsessive. What helped fuel it, of course, was money. I had none. I couldn't afford $15,000 a year for one child especially with four more nipping at my heels. So, I knew I would have to roll up my sleeves and get busy finding the right college, getting my son in it and then making sure I wasn't on the hook for paying more than I could afford.

That's the background. Now, let's return to my son. He wanted a college but where and under what circumstances he didn't know. I checked with other parents. They knew very little and were swayed by what they heard from their contemporaries who knew even less and by the kids of such parents who were in my son's shoes. It was a circle, going nowhere.

I devised a plan. The first thing I did was to find out all the particulars about my own son and his desires. It seemed odd at first, but I soon realized that I knew less about my son than I thought. I compiled a questionnaire which covered all the basic information I needed. You'll see a copy of this questionnaire (known as the Profile) in the Sample Forms section of this book. I had to know what he wanted in a college: Would it be one he commuted to from home, or did he want to live away? If the latter, how far did he want to go? In other words, within three hours driving time or three hours flying time?

Also, did he want cold weather or warm weather? Did he want a coed school and if so, how about the ratio of male to female? Should it be religiously affiliated? How about size? Large, medium or small? What about location? Rural, suburban or urban? Added to these were other questions relating to field of study, extracurricular activities, facilities, social life, and more.

Insofar as cost was concerned, I minimized that. I refused to discount a college simply because its expenses were then beyond my pocketbook. I had been told that there were plenty of scholarships, grants and other financial aid being held by colleges for which no one ever asked. I would ask. Once we settled on a school and were accepted, I felt confident I could get some of their money. Of course, there was one exception here. If my name was Rockefeller, then I wouldn't get anything from a school. Instead, they would be asking me for money. Fortunately (for this purpose only), I wasn't in that category.

I now had an inkling of what my son desired. I took out a map and drew a circle with home as the center, keeping in mind the provisions of the Profile.

I then hit the library.

(I should mention that as an athlete, my son was being contacted directly by a number of colleges which were advising us *not* to go through the admissions office. We were being "forced"—yes, I mean that word—to deal with the athletic departments only. However, I've included a separate section here on the student-athlete that I think you will find most revealing and somewhat disconcerting.)

In any event, I looked up every school in the requested area. You'd be surprised at the number; I was surprised at the number. I had some 65 colleges that seemed to fit the initial bill.

Next stop, I contacted each of them for catalogues, application forms and financial aid information. The postman groaned.

Once the materials started rolling in, we could begin to evaluate—weed out—which ones did not seem appropriate. For example, there was a school that had its buildings divided by a six-lane highway. My son said, "No thanks."

Then, we found one that was "supposed" to be in a rural setting. It was, except for the major jetport sitting a few miles to the left. Or, the school that would only consider a grade point average of 3.7 and SAT scores of at least 1350. We wondered how many students they had who were not named Einstein.

And then there was the school that was totally "dry." No beer, no winc, no parties, no nothing. Just a stringent curfew. very quickly, these schools were discarded and soon we found ourselves with ten left.

Now we come to the next crucial step. How to put the best foot forward? Let me ask you something. Suppose you were given two forms to review, one which is handwritten resembling a pregnant chicken in labor while the other is typewritten? I'll make you a small wager that you'd be prone to look at the one that is easier on the eyes. My son's application would be carefully typed with information presented in a way that would increase the reader's interest.

In fact, I went steps beyond the typewriter. I checked with admissions people at colleges to which we hadn't applied in order to ascertain what they liked to see. Based upon this "expert" advice, I tailor-made the application. We attached a separate biography to supplement what was in the form. We included a flattering snapshot and we arranged for the submission of teacher recommendations...from the good teachers, of course. It was like a military campaign. We even constructed a coherent, well-thought out essay, whether asked for or not. Nothing would be left to chance.

The application materials were sent only to the Director of Admissions, by name, with a request for an interview. We wanted to show we were serious. Such request was granted willingly. Again, returning to my expert advisers, I found out what the interviewers were looking for and grilled my son at length. I even bought him "interview clothes."

With respect to financial aid, I spent literally months turning over every stone. I wanted to find out the best way to file for grants, loans, scholarships and the like. I spent weeks slaving over every aspect and nuance of what other parents termed "the dreaded FAF form." Most never bothered to complete it because of its complexities, or because they erroneously thought they didn't qualify. But, I became the master of it, admittedly no easy feat. I refused to believe there wasn't money to be had.

The bottom line was that my son received acceptances to all ten schools and was awarded considerable financial aid from seven of them. The final step was evaluation and the decision of which offer to accept, a nice position to be in.

I was delighted with this result but was it only as fluke? Was I simply experiencing beginner's luck?

I tried it all again with child number two who had a much lower grade point average, terrible SAT scores and little in the way of extra-curricular activities. Result? Another ten schools applied to—different ones. This time we got nine acceptances (she didn't play football or wrestle) and financial aid from seven of them.

I kept going. The original plan was being fine-tuned and polished. More kids, more schools, more acceptances, more money. High school guidance counselors began contacting me. College admissions people were calling me as to prospective students for the institutions. Friends and relatives came to me as if I were a guru. What to do with all this information?

"There's a worthwhile book here," said my wife, who was born and educated in Europe, and is totally unfamiliar with my modus operandi. "I don't understand the college system in America but you seem to be doing something nobody else can. Why not share it?"

Why not?

And so, here is a step-by-step, easy-to-read, easy-to-digest review of the entire subject. I will even go over the forms with you line-by-line; in effect, we'll do it together.

How to find, get in and pay for the Right College? No problem. Here we go. First stop. Finding the best college.

Chapter 1

FINDING THE RIGHT COLLEGE

When to Begin Looking

When should you begin the search for a college? This is quite different from simply thinking about it. Why? Because many parents begin talking up college as soon as the baby is born.

"Those shoulders. He'll follow in his Dad's footsteps on the field at Penn State's Beaver Stadium."

"Oh, look at those beautiful feet. She'll be a cheerleader. Absolutely. And probably a Miss America. All the best Miss Americas come from Ole Miss anyway."

"I never went to college but my boy will. He'll be the first Mexican-American in the family to attend college. He'll be a Trojan here at USC. I'll be mighty proud, I will."

"Look at that chin. He'll definitely attend Yale."

Huh?

In addition, many families today start early in putting aside a nest egg in the hope that it will cover college expenses some eighteen years hence. Unfortunately, with the rate of inflation being what it has become, there are going to be a few shekels missing when the time comes to pay the piper.

Other parents take different tacts. I know one who made application in his son's name at his own alma mater the day of birth. Oh, not a real application in the sense and form you will see here but a letter to the President of the University and Director of

Admissions requesting a place for his offspring in the class of 2010. He even sent a deposit. Now, that's planning far ahead. I just hope, for his sake, that his son agrees with the choice.

So, in answer to the question, thinking about college can come at any time but actually planting the shovel into the ground should start when your child reaches the junior year of high school.

For ease of understanding, I am, hereinafter, going to talk to the parent. If you're a student reading this, forgive me. I am simply trying to deconfuse the parties. It's like referring to "he/she." It's far easier to use one gender but making sure the reader is aware that the word applies to both. Thus, if you are a student, rest assured that this book is directed at you, as well. After all, the student is the one going to college and everybody else attends vicariously.

The junior year is of prime importance for the student. Of course, all the years preceding are important and you should be encouraging your child to hit those books in order to acquire as high an average as possible. In particular, the junior year is extremely vital as colleges will zero-in on the grades accumulated in that third year of high school. Keep in mind too, that colleges will send out acceptances mid-way through the student's senior year; therefore, good junior year grades become essential. Accordingly, the child must realize that a lot is riding on his success *prior* to the final year.

There are a couple of other elements to consider here along with the grades. For one, make sure the student has double-checked with his adviser on whether there are enough credits to graduate and enter college. And, don't wait until the last semester to do this. It may be too late as happened to one child I know. She was missing a single credit in physical education (gym) and could not graduate with her class that June. I agree it's stupid but...

Secondly, make sure that your child has taken the appropriate college entrance examinations. There are two that are given and most colleges require one or the other.

The Scholastic Aptitude Test (SAT) is a three-hour exam to measure the student's ability to do college work. Part of the test deals with verbal skills such as reading with understanding, using words correctly, and reasoning with them. This section also consists of multiple choice questions designed to test the student's understanding of what they read and the extent of their vocabulary. It includes testing the student's ability to write clearly and correctly as well as competence in the use of the basic rules of grammar and sentence structure. There is also a mathematics section which measures the ability to use and reason with numbers or mathematical concepts. These cover the ability to solve problems involving arithmetical reasoning, algebra and geometry.

The Preliminary Scholastic Aptitude Test (PSAT) is a shortened version of the SAT. It is a 100-minute multiple choice examination that measures verbal and mathematical ability.

The American College Testing Program (ACT) consists of four tests of general educational development covering English usage, mathematics, social studies and natural sciences.

The high school should be able to tell the student when the tests are given but in the event a registration form is not available at the school, or additional information is needed, write to the College Entrance Examination Board at either Box 592, Princeton, New Jersey 08451, or Box 1025, Berkeley, California 94701, regarding the SAT and to P.O. Box 414, Iowa City, Iowa 52240 for the American College Testing Program examination.

Incidentally, the PSAT is generally given at the beginning of the junior year. Make sure it is taken. It will serve as a barometer of what the child may do on the actual SAT and will help you decide whether tutoring may be necessary. The SAT itself is usually given at the end of the junior year. Obviously, that too must be taken. If the scores are low, see that the student retakes the examination as soon as possible. The highest of the scores will be reported to the colleges of your choice. Incidentally, we'll be going through those scores and what they mean later on in this chapter.

Where to Find Help

By the end of the junior year, you should be in the position of beginning the actual hunt for the right college. By this time too, your child may be telling you about some college fairs in your area. The National College Fair is sponsored by the National Association of College Admissions Counselors. It's like a giant trade show where tables and booths are staffed by representatives of various colleges around the country. Counselors and admissions officers will be able to answer questions about college planning, campus life, programs and application procedures. Your child should go to them. He will pick up a lot of information on a wide range of schools which will be helpful in selecting the right college.

Incidentally, there is plenty of information available in your library. I have included within the pages of this book a listing of those publications I consider the best of the lot.

You can also find information about college life in general, and colleges in particular, by talking to the student's adviser, or teachers or friends or relatives. The only thing you have to be careful of is not confusing yourself. The more people you go to, the more convoluted the picture can get.

Usually, the first stop is the school's guidance counselor. However, a word of caution. Guidance counselors can do just so much. More often, they are overworked and underpaid. Therefore, the time and extent of their services are limited.

You can't depend on the students too much, either. Their frame of reference is limited. They talk to their friends who also may have a narrow field of vision (primarily because of their lack of knowledge) or they talk to a relative who knows the school he went to and nothing more.

I still maintain that the best way is for you to take the initiative and use all these other people simply as supplements. Accordingly, if you'll follow the procedures set forth in the succeeding pages, I think you'll be pleasantly surprised at how much easier and more rewarding this entire subject will be. Besides, your child will be going to a school that he really wants based upon his own desires, instead of what somebody else may want.

With the preliminaries now out of the way, it's time to begin focusing on the student himself. Let's find out more about him and, as a result, the school he really seeks.

Type of School

The basic question. What type of school does the student want? It is not as simple as it might appear. Most of the time, there is mass confusion and students will often bounce from one answer to another. Today, they may talk about going to "X" college because Kim is going there. Tomorrow, it is "Y" college because Michael's going there. And then, of course, there is the student who has a C-average, scored below the national norm on the SAT, and has dreams of enrolling in Harvard.

Therefore, your task will be to try and instill some practicality into the matter and at the same time, clear away the cobwebs. Isn't that the function of a parent anyway? Last September, I lectured to a high school graduating class of 450 and discovered that three-fourths of those students had no idea of what was really happening. Many of them were applying to schools because a friend was or because college was considered "the thing to do." Most had few choices; they applied to one or two schools and then crossed their fingers hoping they would not be rejected.

I spoke with a number of parents and they felt they were in the same boat. Unfortunately, their own lack of time, energy and expertise didn't help matters either.

Thus, in order to determine what you can realistically do for your child, you will need to obtain as much information as possible. That's the reason I devised a breakdown sheet on the student. I call it simply the Profile. (See Sample Forms section.) Let's review it line-by-line:

The Profile

Line A: Refers to sex, pure and simple. I like to start with this question as it gets your teenager's immediate attention. You're asking whether your child wants a coed school. Keep in mind, though, that many schools, which were once the domain of one gender, have been desexed—so to speak—and now admit those of the opposite gender. Therefore, unless you have a child who is interested in a school of one sex only (and I don't mean your son's interest in matriculating at an all-girls school), most of the answers will be "Yes." However, if the choice is an all-male or all-female school, then you will quickly see when you begin reviewing colleges, that the selection will be rather limited; in other words, there are few celibacy places left.

What follows next to this is the ratio. Although most schools try to maintain a 50/50 percentage between male and female, this is not always possible. What you may be trying to determine is whether your daughter might be happy at a school where the females outnumber the males 4-1. Obviously, if she was queen of the high school class and voted prettiest, she won't care, but if she never had a date before and is considered just "plain," then such a lopsided ratio might prove to be a hindrance.

Line B: First things first. Does the student want to commute to school and live at home, or does he want to live on a campus? This is a highly personal issue. I, for one, went to school away from home and loved every minute of it. I think it was a good, healthy experience that enabled me to get on my feet faster and with more independence. However, not all kids thrive in such an environment. Some need, or want, to be at home, and you must respect this wish. In fact, of my four who went to college, two commuted and two went away.

Many parents think that money itself determines whether a child goes away to school or stays at home in what's called the commuter or "suitcase" college. It doesn't. When you start applying for financial aid, you will see that the at-home college will base some of its determination on *your* costs beyond tuition.

For example, in New York City, a school like Baruch will estimate that it costs you some $4200 a year to house and feed your child. Therefore, if the tuition is $1800, the college estimates that your cost for the school year is approximately $6000. You see, they take into account the costs of your providing room and board. The school reasons that once the child is 18, he is emancipated under the law and therefore (barring handicapped or incompetent children), your financial responsibility as a parent ends.

Following this further, if you decide to send the child to a state university campus, the cost for tuition, room and board (as of this writing) is around $6000—in effect, the same amount. Thus, if you think you are saving money by keeping thc child at home, think again. You may not be. (See also Chapter 5 on customary first year expenses)

Of course, we are not comparing private schools with their $15,000-a-year price tags, but everything being equal, there may not be such a saving in having your offspring commute to school.

Naturally, the decision on this is not solely yours; it's the student's. Perhaps he's not ready to leave the house yet, or maybe he is. If he has no idea of what a college looks like, then you might want to visit at least one of each: the school that he would commute to and the school where he would live on campus.

If his inclination is towards the latter, then you must ascertain how far away he wants to go. Some parents prefer their kids to be within a few hours driving time of home "in case of emergencies." Some students want to be "as far away as possible."

Needless to say, all this distance depends somewhat on the weather as well. Does the child want to live in a warm or cool climate? For instance, one student I know living in Portland, Maine, wanted a hot weather environment but he also wanted to be within two hours driving time of his home. No such luck. And then there's the student in Miami who wants to ice skate in the winter but also needs to be near her boyfriend who lives next door. Can she really go to Minnesota?

At this point, you have already seen the choices being automatically narrowed. If the student has opted to stay at home, then the colleges you have are now dictated by that decision. If the student wants to go away but wants to be within two hours driving time, the choices are also limited. Of course, the student who says "I don't care, anywhere in the U. S. of A.," presents a still open book. Him you strangle. But, as you will see, that book can be closed somewhat.

Line C: Query. Does the student want a small, medium or large school and does he want it in a rural, suburban or urban setting? When we speak of a small school, we're talking about a student body of under 2,000, not the size or number of the buildings. You won't find a campus with 111 buildings and an auditorium seating 11,000 when the total student population is 1100.

Conversely, don't expect to see a solo building of four floors serving 30,000 students unless it's two miles wide.

Basically, a small school is considered as one in which, as I said, the student body is under 2,000. A medium-sized school usually has a population of 2500-10,000 and the large schools are upwards of that.

Naturally, there are pros and cons relating to these schools. Generally, it is said, although not true in every instance, that a college with a small enrollment tends to have a better faculty-student ratio, meaning the number of teachers to students. For example, one teacher for every 12 students is deemed a good ratio. On the other hand, it is claimed that larger schools are less personal, especially with lecture halls that seat 500. Don't forget that these are all generalities and do not necessarily apply right on down the line.

By the same token, larger schools will usually have more facilities than the smaller ones. A Michigan State will have a library of 1.5 million volumes and will stay open all day and all night while a Juniata College will have a library of 190,000 volumes but might close at 10 p.m.

The bottom line really has to do with the environment in which your child either works best, or desires. Some students function better in a large, high pressure atmosphere while others like a smaller, more personal experience. This is up to the individual and only your child can tell you what he prefers.

The second part of this section deals with the actual location of the college. Does your child want to be in an urban, suburban or rural area? Obviously, if you live in a major city and the student wants to commute to school, the answer is self-apparent. It'll be an urban setting; however, note that many times there are colleges within commuting distance that are right smack in the suburbs. In the New York area, there are schools in the heart of Manhattan and then there are those out on suburban Long Island; and in nearby New Jersey, some even in rural areas. Again, this is a personal preference and you might want to visit some of the schools in each locale to determine what the student may desire.

Each has its advantages and disadvantages depending on the student's point of view. One may feel an advantage in going to Columbia University and being in New York City.

"You have all of the Big Apple right around you," said one freshman.

To another student, this was a drawback.

"Hell, you're caught in the center of a hurricane which is not conducive to good study habits."

That same student might enjoy the peace and tranquility of a school in the middle of Iowa while the former might find it downright boring "talking to corn fields all day."

Line D: This may or may not be important to the student. Most colleges in the private sector have connections to a church or other religious group. Think Notre Dame and you think Catholic. Think B.Y.U. and you think Mormon. Think Brandeis or Yeshiva and you think Jewish. Think S.M.U. and it's Methodist.

The fact is that except for a handful of schools, the religious aspect today has been minimized considerably. It's certainly not prevalent in state schools.

Take a private college like St. John's on Long Island in New York. Good basketball teams, eh? Obviously, with a name like St. John's, most people wouldn't exactly consider it a branch of Tel Aviv University. Yet, this Roman Catholic school with the large cross on its main building has a hefty Jewish student body. This highly-rated academic institution does not force religion down the student's throat like compelling him to mass every day. The only requirement is that a course in theology must be taken and the choice of religion to study is a wide one. You can concentrate on Hindu, if you wish.

The decision to have any religious studies is, again, something for both you and the student to discuss.

Line E: We now come to the real reason your child is going to college—to pursue a certain course of study. By now, the student should have an idea, albeit a general one, as to what he may want to do with his life. Some know they want to be doctors or lawyers or engineers or teachers; some are undecided. This latter group is all too common. A good 40% of the students entering college have not decided on any specific major. In fact, once in college, almost 50% of the freshman class will change their major field of study by the time they enter the second year. So, don't fret if your offspring doesn't have a goal in mind right now. Actually, it may work in the student's favor in order to get into certain schools. (I'll go into that aspect in greater detail when we discuss the application forms.)

But, bear in mind that the more you can nail down the specifics, or at least be able to rule out certain areas, the better off you will be in trying to determine the right college.

For instance, the Massachussets Institute of Technology is an extraordinary school but you wouldn't normally pick it to study pre-law. Similarly, you wouldn't go to an Allegheny College, which is a well-respected liberal arts school, to study advanced engineering.

Furthermore, why send a music major to a school that has only two courses in music when there are schools like Oberlin which has a conservatory of music. Then too, a student interested in music may find that the University of Texas at Austin will have a marching band, a symphony orchestra, a string quartet and a theatre group, while the much smaller Lynchburg College in Virginia won't have a marching band because it doesn't have a football team, yet the music department there provides courses and areas of instruction in music-business that its big brother to the southwest does not have.

Line F: A rather large area that will mean more to the student than it will to you. Find out what your child is interested in outside of the classroom. If she has had experience on the high school newspaper and wants to extend that experience to college, then you must make sure that the school selected has a student newspaper. The same holds true for other activities: radio stations, theatre groups, music ensembles, fraternities, sororities, language clubs, camera clubs and the like. Even for the athlete, it's important. A boy who wants to try out for the volleyball team better be at a school that plays volleyball; not all do.

Line G: This is known as the Grade Point Average, or GPA. You have to know the student's average to-date. Granted it doesn't include the senior year for the student hasn't completed that yet, but as I said earlier, schools will notify students of acceptances or rejections around the start of the second semester of the senior year. Their decisions are based on grades through the junior year although some schools will also include the first semester of the senior year (known as the mid-term marking period).

Understanding what the student's average is and what it means will go a long way toward scaling down the number of colleges to be selected. For example, it would be foolish to apply to a place like Stanford if the student has a D+ average. Although I am basically an optimist and rarely take "No" for an answer. I am also a realist. A student with a downright lousy academic record shouldn't waste time and money applying to schools for which the response will be obvious.

Line H: Here you should include the scores from all entrance examinations. Most often it will be the Scholastic Aptitude Test (SAT), and its numbers will give you an idea of your chances at specific schools.

Most colleges give some credence to the scores of the College Board examinations. Many colleges consider the results important because they say it is a scientific way of comparing all candidates with respect to their ability to do college work. They claim that a high school record alone cannot be a yardstick of academic promise.

However, more and more colleges are aware that certain students may not do well on big tests even though they score well in the classroom. While for the time being they are considered important, a good high school record, plus some other extra curricular activities, may offset a poor showing in these standardized tests.

In any event, let me give you an idea of what some colleges consider as their average scores for incoming freshmen. To be sure, this is not a complete list but it will show you what certain schools, at this writing, may be looking for. Bear in mind that with the SAT scores, which is the primary testing service used (more so than ACT), a perfect score on each section (verbal and math) would be 800, or 1600 combined. Average scores last year across the nation were 414 in verbal and 457 in mathematics.

Adelphi	433V, 465M
Allegheny	521V, 563M
Boston College	530V, 552M
Boston University	528V, 567M
Brandeis	580V, 620M
Calif. Institute of Technology	650V, 750M
Clemson	469V, 533M
Colgate	598V, 626M
Cornell	589V, 647M
Dartmouth	650V, 650M
Denison	490V, 520M
Duke	620V, 660M
Duquense	450V, 550M
Fordham	525V, 540M
Georgetown	622V, 646M
Georgia State	455V, 473M
Haverford	650V, 650M
Hollins	471V, 472M
Holy Cross	563V, 587M
Indiana	453V, 491M
Kalamazoo	562V, 589M

Lafayette	560V, 630M
Lewis & Clark	515V, 533M
Marquette	476V, 538M
M.I.T.	625V, 730M
Miami	504V, 558M
Michigan State	470V, 530M
N.Y.U.	545V, 565M
Oberlin	610V, 620M
Ohio	419V, 459M
Oregon State	440V, 495M
Penn State	501V, 563M
Princeton	638V, 672M
Purdue	420V, 470M
Rutgers	492V, 547M
St. John's	450V, 491M
S.M.U.	500V, 550M
Stanford	620V, 670M
Sweet Briar	500V, 500M
Syracuse	512V, 546M
Temple	450V, 450M
Texas A&M	1032 composite
Tufts	580V, 620M
Tulane	520V, 596M
Univ. of Calif. (Davis)	510V, 571M
Univ. of Dayton	467V, 522M
Univ. of Florida	488V, 545M
Univ. of Houston	430V, 480M
Univ. of Maryland	450V, 510M
Univ. of Notre Dame	570V, 640M
Univ. of Rochester	561V, 618M
Univ. of Southern Calif.	484V, 540M
Univ. of Texas	500V, 550M
Univ. of Virginia	585V, 641M
Vanderbilt	568V, 611M
Vassar	580V, 580M
Wake Forest	539V, 548M
Washington & Lee	570V, 585M
Wells	550V, 550M
Yale	670V, 690M

But, here too, one must look at the figures carefully. One of my children applied to Notre Dame. As you can see from the above list, the university sets forth a combined score on the SAT of 1210. That's a hefty number. My son pulled a 980; we've got a hell of a difference.

However, he had a 3.5 grade point average and with his extra curricular involvement, the college reviewed his file a little more closely. Notre Dame, like other schools, is aware that many students freeze-up on standardized tests. The result? My son was accepted. Out of some 8,000 applicants, he was one of the 1300 accepted.

So, you have to do a bit of a balancing act between the Grade Point Average and the SAT. Sometimes a low score in one area may be offset by a high score in another.

Basically, this is the profile you need. Once you have it in hand, then you'll be ready for the next step in your campaign, which is matching the college to the individual.

You're now ready to begin looking at schools. But, what you don't want to do is waste time. Before you start buying books indiscriminately or even contacting those college representatives you might have met at a trade fair, you should decide on an approach to follow. My recommendation is to nail down the location first. Here's what I mean.

With the commuting student, the selection will be considerably smaller than with the on-campus student. In this instance, you have to determine how your child will be commuting to school. If it's by car, then you can ascertain how long he would drive to and from college; accordingly, you will be able to list which schools fall within that driving time. If he's taking public transportation, the area will shrink and if he is walking to and from school, it will narrow even more.

As for the student who wants to go out of town, it won't do you any good to review schools in California if you live in St. Louis and your son wants to be within a few hours driving time of the house. Therefore, based upon his profile as to the desired mileage from the home to school, you can draw a circle on a map with the residence as the center. Obviously, if you live in Washington, D.C. and your child wants to be within three hours of the house but wants a warm weather college, then you will be looking at a 180 degree radius; those areas to the north will be excluded.

The climate factor itself will help exclude certain places while including others. Armed with this information and the Profile, you can then proceed with attacking the source materials.

Now, I should add that you can probably obtain a list of potential colleges from the guidance counselor at the high school. Many high schools (as well as private search companies) have turned to the computer for such information. These computers allegedly match the student's profile to a college. Notice I said "allegedly." It might be adequate for the initial selection purpose, but I have found that many times those lists are too incomplete, primarily because there are too many variables. Although I think my way is not as convenient, it is certainly more rewarding and infinitely more accurate. At the risk of finding men in white coats on my doorstep, I have to tell you that over the past five years, I have actually reviewed material on every single four-year college in the United States, and my advice would be to head for the library or bookstore.

There are plenty of books on the subject of colleges and you can read yourself into a tizzy. But, at this time, you are simply casting a large net out to see what's there to fit the bill. Keep in mind that you're going to contact more schools than you planned, or to which you might eventually apply.

The main books on the subject, in my opinion, are the following:

1) *Barron's Profiles of American Colleges*, published by The Barron's Educational Series. This book offers a breakdown of each college on a state-by-state basis. Thus, if you were looking for schools in the State of North Carolina, this book will have a section devoted to North Carolina and that would list all the colleges within that area. It furnishes information on environment, student life, programs of study, admissions procedures, financial aid, to name a few. This is the book I would recommend.

2) *Lovejoy's College Guide*, published by Simon & Schuster, is similar to Barron's, It also breaks the colleges down on a state-by-state level. It's the second choice.

3) *Comparative Guide to American Colleges*, by Cass & Birnbaum, published by HarperCollins, also affords much the same information as the other two above, but the drawback is that it lists the schools alphabetically and not state-by-state.

4) *Peterson's Four-Year Colleges,* profiles some 2000 colleges in a massive work.

However, once you've decided on certain schools, it's worth looking at some other books for additional information. There are three which do not list all the colleges but are entertaining to read *after* the selection has been narrowed or a decision of which school to accept has to be made.

A) *Selective Guide to Colleges,* by Edward B. Fiske, published by Times Books. This book rates 275 of what Mr. Fiske considers are the best and most interesting four-year institutions in the nation. Basically, they are essays of approximately 600 to 2000 words each. It makes for fascinating reading because it delves into rating the academics of the college, the social environment, the quality of life, plus providing facts on SAT scores, male/female ratios, expenses and how many applicants each school gets, how many are accepted, and how many actually enroll.

B) *The Insiders Guide to the Colleges,* published by St. Martin's Press, is a snapshot of life at over 270 colleges. It covers some of what the Fiske book does but with more emphasis on the physical and social aspects.

C) *Lisa Birnbach's College Book,* published by Ballantine Books. This goes into what she considers the "juicy stuff" such as the cafeteria, clothes, guys, gals. 186 schools are listed and there are various essays with individual interviews.

I would suggest that you use *Barron's* to get the initial selection of schools and that you look first at location. For example, if the desire is for a school within so many miles of home, then you can simply extract from that book all those schools within the state, or within the areas so designated. I wouldn't worry about all the other material right now. You might have a tendency to exclude certain schools based upon their size or environment but I recommend you don't do that here. As you will see later on, you may have to include a few of those schools that don't match the profile exactly in order to have stop-gaps.

But, for the present, the easiest way to limit the search is based on location. In addition, if you read all the materials on a particular college, you might begin to form an opinion, which is fine too, although I suggest that you look at the catalogues and promotional literature before you make any final decision. They may be more up to date and they will most likely have actual photographs of the campus.

Remember the school with the six lane major highway running through it? We never would have known that from the materials in the books. Only when we saw a photograph of the campus did we realize what was going on. Also, you can tell quite a lot about the college from the materials you receive. I know of one well-respected school whose application form was a mimeographed sheet of paper and its catalogue looked as if it had been prepared at the turn of the century. As far as I was concerned, it said something about the professional (or, in this case, unprofessional) way the school operated.

You now should have a list of potential schools. Telephone (many have toll-free numbers) or write these for information. I have found that the best way is simply to send postcards to the Director of Admissions asking for (1) catalogue, (2) application form and (3) financial aid materials. Also, I suggest you keep a list of these contacts so that you know who's responding. As the information comes in, you can then check it off the list.

I would start this initial contact during the summer between the junior and senior years. That's usually a good time to pour over catalogues and begin to get your ducks in line. I would also suggest that you keep all the college materials in one place. You will find that once you have a senior on your hands, you'll begin to receive catalogues and letters from colleges you never heard of, and which aren't on the original selection list. This is par for the course. It's akin to the junk mail you receive.

Don't you ever wonder how the purveyor of electronic garage door openers got your name and address? You live in an apartment building with no garage downstairs yet here comes a brochure addressed to you asking how you could have lived all these years without the new 'EZ Opener Garage Door Keeper.' Selling of mailing lists is big business in this country. Most merchants buy such lists from outfits like American Express, MasterCard, Visa, Diners Club, the oil companies and department stores; in fact, almost anywhere a credit card is used. Even if you register at a hotel and pay cash, your name and address winds up on a list that may be sold to others. So, it is not unusual for colleges to get their paws on similar lists. In fact, students contribute to this wide-spread practice when they attend conferences, seminars or sign up for college fairs, buy class rings, copies of yearbooks, and the like.

Besides, in some instances, I've heard colleges were getting them directly from the high schools. Most amusing, of course, is that the mailings do not discriminate. One of my daughters received an interest from an all-boys school and one of my sons received literature to join the WACS.

Having been exposed to the paper war that pervaded our household, I've found that the most organized way of handling the matter was to keep everything together. Thus, all materials from "X" college would remain inside the mailing envelope and all envelopes would be placed in a big box labeled with the student's name. You will find, especially if your initial contact is to a large number of schools, that it is rather easy to get application form to "Y" college mixed up with the catalogue on "Z" college which has a "T" college's financial aid form attached.

Evaluation of Schools

I think it's fun to pour over college catalogues. It's also rather intriguing and revealing to see what the colleges will send. Most will be slick promotional materials with lots of pictures, all pointing to the school's attributes. Your job then is to evaluate what has been sent. I break this down into two steps.

In the first instance, what you are doing is basically getting rid of the superfluous. For example, if your child is interested in becoming a teacher and you have received a catalogue, unsolicited, from a trade school for automobile mechanics, it would be best to toss that envelope and its contents immediately into the circular file...and I mean immediately. Do not pass go, do not collect two hundred. Who needs to have it clutter up the house? By the same token, if one of the colleges on your list sends in material that is obviously not to the student's liking (for example, a school with heavy religious overtones), then that too should be scrapped. The purpose of the initial evaluation then is to reject those schools in which the student has no interest whatsoever. What you should have left then will be those schools to which some interest is present. The next step is the weeding-out process.

The extent of this depends a great deal on the circumstances. If the student has decided to stay at home and there are only three schools in the commuting area, then your work has been drastically minimized. If, however, the student has given you carte blanche and a wide latitude, you may find yourself with 60 colleges on your hands; accordingly, the process is a little more complicated. In my own situation, working with my children as well as those of friends and relatives, I generally found myself asking for materials from considerably more colleges than necessary. Here is where some creativity comes into play.

Look at it this way. First, you have already decided, based on weather and commuting miles, to retain materials from certain schools. Now you must weed out more of the "No's."

Obviously, the prime area would be course of study. A quick look at the catalogues will answer that question. It does no good to make application to a school that doesn't have the major your child wants, provided, of course, a major has been selected. If it hasn't, you can almost skip this part.

Secondly, look at the size. You might have received materials from schools that fit the profile in all categories except one, like size. Question: how important is that one category? The bottom line is that you want to reduce the numbers on that list appreciably. In my opinion, you are looking to bring this down to ten.

As you can see from my earlier discussion, I am an advocate of not putting all the eggs in one basket but in applying to as many schools as is feasible and within reason. Translated, "within reason," to me, is ten. Granted this is an arbitrary number, but you have to remember that of the ten schools to which applications are made, there may be a few rejections. My own experience in this area shows that after such rejections, you will be left with seven. Then, you will find that of those seven, only three may give you the kind of financial aid you need. This means that the student may be faced with deciding which school to go to among only three choices—three out of an original list of sixty.

That's what this is all about. I believe you need the leeway.

In addition, when I complete the weeding-out process, I generally include in the final ten, a few that were not quite in line with the

Profile. These are known as the "stop-gap" schools.

The best way to explain this is to give you an example. Let's take a friend's son. He wanted a small school, preferably in a suburban or rural location, within five hours driving of home, no preference on climate, wanted coed, good balance male/female, biology major, religion considered unimportant, sports a necessity, school newspaper, fraternity. His GPA was 3.4 and his SAT was 990.

Casting the line out, I came up with some 73 schools. I kid you not. Oh, not all of them fit the Profile exactly but there were a sufficient number that did. Of these ten, five were to his liking. Of the other five, we applied to three state schools, which were larger than he wanted but whose costs were considerably less than the first five which were all private institutions sporting $12,000-a-year price tags. The three state schools were our stop-gaps in case we couldn't get the aid we needed from any of the first five. We felt confident too that he would have no trouble getting into these three.

The remaining two were, to a certain extent, based on the colleges themselves. We made application to one because there was an athletic interest there and because the son's father had gone there. We applied to another simply because of their interest in the student although it had a huge student body and was more than five hours driving time of home.

So, what we did was split the vote. We applied to a number of schools that were line with the student's wishes, a few which we felt sure he could get into and which we could pay for if everything else turned to sawdust and a couple that were really outside the student's basic interest.

What happened? The student was accepted to all ten schools and saw decent financial aid from seven of those schools.

Once you have decided on those to which applications are going to be made, I strongly suggest that you make the second of the charts (yes, I am chart-happy). Again, this is a simple form but you will find it most helpful. It's aptly called the Flow Chart and it's included in the Sample Forms section of this book. As you can see, it's self-explanatory and you need only to fill in the blanks. I can't tell you how many people miss one deadline or another because of a disorganized approach to college.

I made this chart and affixed it to the refrigerator door so that everybody in the household was fully aware of where we were in the application process and what still had to be done.

Thus, if I or the student failed to note something on the chart, chances were good that someone else in the house would pick it up and remind us. We were all in this together and it worked like a charm. In effect, it was one huge followup/tickler file.

Chapter 2

GETTING INTO THE RIGHT COLLEGE

At this point, you should have the final list of colleges to which applications are going to be made. Now, before you rush pell-mell into filling out the forms, signing your application checks and sending in materials, I suggest that you consider the campaign on a first-things-first basis. We start with:

The Application Form

Initially,what you want to do is review each application form by itself, one college at a time, in order to decide exactly what you must complete...*and when.*

Take out the Flow Chart from the Sample Forms section. It's time to start filling in the blanks. I suggest that you line up the colleges separately. Eventually, you will list them on the chart. But work in order of priority. For example, suppose you have five colleges. These should all be listed on the chart with a checkmark in the second column indicating whether the appropriate information (catalogue, application form, financial aid form, transcript form), have all been received. It's important that this be addressed for there are instances when a college only sends out an initial packet of information, or "feeler," about its school but waits to hear from the prospective applicant as to whether additional materials are desired. With costs being what they are, it is not surprising that some schools will only send catalogues (which are quite expensive to produce), when they are sure there is more than a fleeting interest. So, be certain that you have received the necessary materials.

Next is perhaps the most important column of all: the application deadline.

You must know exactly when that application is to be on file at the college. That's why I recommend going through each college's materials and putting them in chronological order on the Flow Chart. List those colleges first which have the earliest application deadlines. This way you can move down the list filing the forms in proper order. It lessens the chances of missing a deadline.

Now, turning to the form itself, I suggest that you take one application—one school at a time—so that you don't mix them up. You will find that most forms request the same information although the color of the paper, type-face, position of questions, will differ. Some schools, especially large state institutions, are computerized so that you may be confronted with darkening circles rather than actually listing information.

You should make a photocopy of each application form, the intention being to prepare a draft, in pencil, before you transpose the information to the original. Too often, people start right in with the form and by the time they are done, it is replete with changes: erasures, white-outs, cross-outs, and the like. You don't want this. You want a neat, clean form when completed. And, as I mentioned in the Introduction, it would be best to have it typewritten. I've spoken to enough admissions officers to know that they like application forms that are easy on the eyes and preferably those that are not folded every which way to Sunday. So, if you want to give them what they really want, and make a lasting impression, your application form should be typewritten and sent in a large, flat envelope.

I've enclosed what is known as a common application form as an example. (Actually, it's the one from Gettysburg College.) A number of schools recommend this form. You'll see some of them printed at the top of the form's face page. The idea is to inject some uniformity into the application process. That's why it's called a Common Application form. Those colleges listed, plus a number of others, believe that this concept will save a lot of time, money and energy. It does.

To show you how the form should be completed, I've taken a fictitious name and address. So, let's begin.

Put the photocopy of your application next to your writing hand,

and this Common Form either to the right or left of it. This book can be in front of you, if you wish. If the form you are working on is different, simply make the adaptations. I recommend that you and your child do this together. I know, I know. "The student is supposed to do it all." I realize that but as far as I am concerned, I believe that two good heads are better than one, and you want to do everything possible to get an acceptance here. Therefore, you work as a team. Keep in mind that when the form is completed, an application check will accompany it (***non-refundable***), so you'll have some dough riding on the line.

The first section is "Personal Data." I don't think this needs much explanation. You will see that it covers the essential stuff. If your child is from a divorced family such as in the example shown, then simply insert the different addresses. The college people understand what all these different addresses mean and you will find them most cooperative in making sure that information is disseminated to all parties concerned.

Now, one interesting part has to do with the matter of academic concentration. Does the student declare the field of study at this time?

It depends. There is a trick here and it's perfectly legitimate. The student may or may not want to declare a major this early. Let me explain.

There has been a plethora of students applying for the schools of business. The business major has taken over as the primary one at most colleges. That means competition. That also means you must be creative. Most colleges have quotas on its various majors. For argument's sake, a particular school might have four areas of study: business, communications, science, health services. (I know, it's a pretty small school and rather limited, but we're only using it as an example.) Now, suppose that school can accept 400 people into its freshman class. It establishes a quota for each area of study. In the business school, it has room for 150, in communications it will take 100, in science it will take 50 and in health services it will take 25. That adds up to 325, leaving 75 places open for what is called the "Undeclared" category.

If, out of 1500 applicants for admission, 500 are applying for the school of business, there is no question but that 350 of them will not get in...and I don't mean simply the school of business. They won't be accepted to that college...period! And, among those 350, there may be plenty with decent grades and decent SAT scores.

Therefore, you and the student must do a little homework. If you are applying for a major that attracts a large number of applicants (the catalogue will tell you this as well as the *Barron's* book from the preceding chapter), and your child's grades and SAT scores are simply so-so, with no special extra curricular activities to bolster the position, then you might want to put down "Undeclared" instead of a specific major. In other words, if only 80 students in a freshman class list "Undeclared" and the school can take 75, your child will have a better chance of getting into the college under this category. Remember, the key here is to secure an acceptance into the school. Once there, the student can make changes in the major area of study. Statistics support the fact that almost 50% of the freshmen change their majors at the end of the first year.

Now, understand that I am not suggesting you do this in all instances, but it is certainly something of which you should be aware.

Incidentally, you will note a place for a social security number. Most colleges use this as the basic identification system for the application form, financial aid and the like. Thus, if your child doesn't have such a number, I suggest that he/she obtains one. Simply contact your local social security office for details. It will also help facilitate financial aid as some of the aid is given for a work-study program; that requires the social security number for payment. No big deal here, but just an added sidelight that should be considered.

Some parents have asked me about the section on describing yourself; in other words, as being part of a particular race or ethnic group. Many people get disturbed over this. Frankly, I wouldn't. I have spoken with enough admissions people and enough college presidents to know that little attention is paid to this area. It's primarily a question for demographic record-keeping. Oh, sure, there are certain schools that may like to keep their campuses pristine within a certain race, but which will every now and then pick up a minority or "token" student. However, except for those isolated colleges (and who would want to go there anyway?), most gloss over this answer. Instead, they look for a good balance of students in all areas...and rightfully so. I wouldn't agonize about this question but would concentrate on other parts that make more sense: good grades, good SATs, extra-curricular activities, essays, interviews...all carrying much greater weight.

Under "Educational Data," you will note that there is a CEEB Code Number. This is the high school's code number and you can get that directly from them.

Moving right along, we come to "Test Information." Here, they are asking about the SAT results. If you have them, you can insert the scores; if not, simply advise when the test will be taken. If the test that was taken proved rather low, then insert a date showing when the next one will be taken. Colleges recognize that most students don't take the test once and simply report that result, especially if it is not good. The idea is to retake the test as many times as you want, to obtain the highest score possible. That's the score that will be reported.

The section on "Family" is self-explanatory. Try to include as much as you can. Don't stint, and of course, if there are others in the family, give their names and ages. Colleges like to know of any brothers or sisters who may be potential recruits for the school. It doesn't hurt.

"Academic Honors" must be carefully thought through. Find out everything you can about the student. What the student may think is unimportant may impress an admissions officer. The same holds true for extracurricular and personal activities. Leave no stone unturned. Ask the student to list everything, grade by grade. You'd be surprised at what usually begins with "I've done nothing" soon evolves into a number of different honors, awards and activities.

"I've done nothing in high school. I wasn't on any athletic teams and I wasn't in the student government."

"What did you do during your first year of high school?"

"Oh, nothing much."

"Belong to any clubs?"

"Nah, only a fraternity."

"Did the fraternity take part in any community service?"

"Like?"

"Like helping to raise money for charity, blood drives. That like."

"Oh, yeah, I remember, we had a big blood drive. Got a lot of people, too."

"What was your position with it?"

"Oh, just the chairman with somebody else. But we certainly did a lot for the hospital."

Hah! Paydirt.

Or...

"Belong to any clubs?"

"Like what?"

"Camera club, language club."

"Nah, only the debating club."

"Debate other schools?"

"Yeah."

"Did you win?"

"I guess so. Nobody ever beat me. But that was only for two years."

Bingo again!

See what I mean? Probe, dig and you'll find. Add them here—all of them—no matter how silly they may sound. You've got to stack up the ammunition.

The same applies to "Work Experience." Again, don't stint and don't be afraid to include everything, even though you might consider it demeaning.

"Oh, she worked at Burger King one summer."
Nothing wrong with that. Put it in. It shows a willingness to work. Don't be embarrassed, don't be ashamed. It's better than a kid who does nothing but watch television after school. The admissions people want to see enterprise; they don't want to see laziness. They like hard workers.

We now come to the "Personal Statement." Some applications will ask for this; some will not. Many state institutions are computerized and will not request an essay.
My opinion is to include essays in all applications, and I mean *all* applications, whether asked for or not. Keep in mind that you want to throw in as many things in your favor as possible.

I've heard parents and students saying, "Why give them something they haven't asked for? Why volunteer information?" Hey, this isn't the army. You're trying to get *into* something, not out of it.

Some parents and students claim it's pretentious. "It's too pushy." Really? Who cares? Again, you're trying to nail down an acceptance. You want to show aggressiveness—yes, pushiness—to a certain extent. *You want to show you're interested.*

Don't be concerned about other applicants. You should be concerned about your child, making sure you've got all the necessary guns in place. Believe me, they won't backfire.

You will note that I don't limit an essay to the blank space on the form. The sample student wrote two of them and we included both. Now, for those editors, writers and Nobel Prize winners out there, take it easy. Here is where you have to back off somewhat. Don't wind up writing the essays for your child. Admissions people are not stupid. They know instantly when something has been written by an eighteen-year old, no matter how bright, and when the parent's expert hand has been inserted. If you want to clean up some spelling, okay, but let the basic thoughts and grammatical construction stay as is. There aren't that many eighteen-year olds who can write error-free anyway. In other words, step aside and let it go. You want to help, fine, but watch out. I've known parents who, under the guise of being helpful, suggest fifty dollar words to bolster the essay. Don't you think the admissions people can spot such aid a million miles away?

Finally, some creativity. Add photographs where appropriate and certainly a good snapshot of the student.

The application is now complete...in rough. Double-check the information (you'd be surprised at how many mistakes you'll pick up on the second go-round) before you head toward the typewriter. (I still suggest a typewriter unless someone in the family can print extremely well.)

When the application is ready, the student should sign and date it. Then, attach a check covering the filing fee to the face page and prepare to mail.

Incidentally, one thing about the fee. Keep in mind that it's going to cost between $20-50 for each college and they are basically non-refundable fees except under certain circumstances due to hardship. (In fact, most colleges will waive the fee in the event of hardship cases.) Make sure the fee is in check form. DO NOT SEND CASH. And, mark the bottom of the check with the student's name and social security number. Also, and most importantly, double check your bank balance so that you have funds to cover the fee. I kid you not. Bounced checks do not exactly present a good image.

In addition, I suggest a covering note to the Director of Admissions. It should be simple, straight-forward, like this:

Mr. John J. Smith
Director of Admissions
Favorite College
0000 College Way
Collegetown, U.S.A. 00000

Dear Mr. Smith:

I am enclosing my completed application form for the freshman class beginning with the 1992 fall semester, together with the filing fee.

The additional materials to complete the file will be forthcoming.

Thank you for your courtesy and cooperation.

Sincerely,

Stuart S. Student

Needless to say, the covering letter is from the student, not you.

Once this is complete, make a photocopy of the form for your files and send the original, with the correct postage, to the college. Don't worry about the transcripts, teacher recommendations, SAT scores, etc., right now. The idea is to get the application form into the school so that a file on your child can be opened. Believe me, the college will keep you apprised of missing materials but it can't do so until it has an actual file in place.

Now, turn back to the Flow Chart and insert the date the application was filed.

Okay, final question. When to file? I suggest around October-November of the student's senior year.

With the application form now out of the way, we can then turn to the other items necessary to complete the application process. First off, the...

Transcript

Along with the application form, the college will send you a sheet that is to be given to the student's high school guidance counselor who will complete and return same to the admissions office. In effect, the college is asking that the guidance counselor review the student's high school record and submit a transcript of the grades (plus grade point average) including a verification as to the student's standing in the class. This is done between the high school and the college with neither you nor the child being involved in any way.

Some colleges may send the transcript requests separate from the application form; others may have it as part of the form. In any event, the procedure is simply to turn the request over to the high school, asking them to submit the proper materials to the college. If the request for the transcript information is attached to the application form or made a part of it, then you must, of course, submit the entire form to the high school guidance counselor.

I suggest the following procedure when dealing with transcripts:

First, let's suppose the transcript request is separate from the application form. Then, attach to each request a return-addressed envelope made out to the Director of Admissions at the particular college, with proper postage affixed.

Secondly, put all the transcript request forms in one folder with the student's name on the cover and have the student deliver them personally to the guidance counselor accompanied by a covering letter asking that the forms be completed and returned to the colleges as soon as convenient. Explain in the letter that all the envelopes have been prepared and postage has been added. Of course,do thank the guidance counselor for his/her courtesy and cooperation.

You will need that cooperation. Remember, once the college submission gets into full swing, the guidance counselor will be swamped with transcript request forms. Frankly, what you are trying to do is curry some favor. By putting everything in one folder, by having the envelopes already made out and affixing the proper postage, you are attempting to ease the guidance counselor's work. I don't know of any counselor who wouldn't appreciate this help. As a result, by helping the person you desperately need, you are helping yourself. As you can readily see, it cuts both ways.

And, at the risk of sounding totally mercenary, a good guidance counselor is invaluable in getting the file completed sooner and thereby assisting in securing an early (and hopefully more favorable) response from the student's college of choice.

I also believe in acknowledging the guidance counselor's help by thanking him/her in writing for the courtesies extended. A copy should be sent to the principal of the school and to the superintendent of the district, as well.

Incidentally, the same procedure applies where the application form is part of the transcript request. However, in this regard, I would suggest your making a copy of the application form and sending that to the college together with a covering note explaining that the original of the form is with the guidance counselor. Once more, you are making every effort to have a file opened on the student. You can't afford to turn in an application/transcript form to the guidance counselor on October 1st and find that because of the deluge of requests, the counselor was unable to send the materials to the college until November 15th. During that six week interval, you could at least have the application file set up by the college.

Don't forget that there are just so many places in any freshman class and if the particular college has an enormous number of applicants (for example, like Brown University did last year with some 11,717 applicants to fill about 2,000 places), you want to get a jump on admissions.

In addition, there are early admissions procedures (which we will discuss later on) that reduce the available openings.

Once the transcript materials have been submitted to the guidance counselor, then you can check-mark the space on the Flow Chart; however, you also must maintain a followup file in order to monitor the forwarding of transcript materials. I would "tickle" the matter for approximately three weeks and then I would drop a note to the college asking whether or not the transcript information has been received. If not, then you can always go to the guidance counselor to ascertain the reasons for the delay.

Once the college acknowledges receipt of these materials, then you can add a slash through the checkmark signifying such receipt and completion.

Teacher Recommendations

The same procedure generally applies with this aspect of the application process. You will probably find that included in the application package will be sheets headed "Teacher Recommendation." These are usually not attached to the forms themselves but will be separate pieces of paper. Not all schools require this but a goodly number do.

The modus operandi here is for the student to take these forms to the respective teachers of his or her choice for completion and return directly to the colleges. There will generally be two recommendations required. The strategy is pretty much the same as with the transcripts. All of these recommendation forms should be accompanied by a return envelope, addressed to the Director of Admissions at the particular college, and they should all have the proper postage affixed. You can't expect teachers to write down their opinions of the student and then have to worry about finding envelopes, addressing them and paying for postage. After all, *they* are the ones extending the favor.

Needless to say, it would be best to check with the teacher first as to whether he/she would be willing to write a recommendation. If cleared, then I suggest you put all the required forms together in one folder—the same as was done with the transcripts—for delivery to the specific teachers.

With respect to what teachers should be selected, the answers are rather obvious. You are looking for the best recommendations possible; thus, it doesn't really do much good to pass the form on to a teacher in whose class the student was failing or has a rather low grade average. You should use those teachers where the student is doing his best work; common sense dictates that favorable recommendations would come from that teacher.

But another aspect should be considered as well. This concerns dovetailing the recommendation to the student's major. For example, if the student is declaring engineering as his major, then it would be worthwhile to have recommendations from those teachers in the science/technology field.

Conversely, the effect is minimized by having a recommendation from a history teacher. So, all things being equal, a recommendation for the engineering student should come from a mathematics or science teacher which would, in my opinion, hold more weight than a recommendation from one teaching human sexuality.

The same holds true for the kinds of teachers. Obviously, those of major academic positions (English, Math, History, Science) will be considered more seriously than the gym or health teacher (all due respects extended).

Therefore, the idea is to find the best teachers to support the student.

Also, it is unimportant if those teachers are not all teaching junior or senior year subjects. If the student did rather well in a subject in prior years (like the tenth grade), there is no problem in using that teacher here as a reference. However, I draw the line at going back to elementary school.

Again, as with the transcripts, once the forms are delivered to the teachers, you can check-mark the space on the Flow Chart. A followup should be maintained in about four weeks (teachers are notoriously slower in replying than guidance counselors), and, of course, don't be shy in thanking the teacher for the efforts made.

We now come to the area that is a little more tricky and which requires close scrutiny to procedure. We deal with the...

SAT Scores

As you can readily see, the work load does not ease any. Of course, I don't believe I ever said it would. This is exactly the reason why many students do not get into the college they necessarily should or want, and do not receive the financial aid they are entitled to. It takes some effort to complete the application process correctly but in my opinion the rewards at the end will be worth it.

The College Board Scholastic Aptitude Tests are generally given in January, April, May, June, October, November and December. I suggest that the test first be taken in May. Scores will be sent back within three to four weeks. Incidentally, for the original price of admission, the student can have the test scores sent to three colleges. So, as long as you're paying for the tests anyway (usually around $15), you may as well have the reports sent to at least three colleges on your list.

Of course, if you're worried about the results and prefer to wait and see how good they are, then you may pass on having them sent at this time. In any event, once you decide to send them, you should pick up what is called an Additional Report Request Form. The guidance office in your high school should have them; if not, write to The College Board, Box 592-A, Princeton, New Jersey 08541. They're free.

The Additional Report Request Form is machine-processed.

Thus, with a Number 2 pencil, you fill in the requested information in each row of boxes. A listing of the various college codes is also enclosed here.

Once the forms are completed, you return them along with the appropriate fee to the College Board. In that respect, I recommend a covering letter, as follows:

> College Board
> ATP
> Box 592-A
> Princeton, NJ 08541
>
> Gentlemen: Re: (Student's Name & ID Number)
>
> Enclosed herewith are_____Additional Report Request Forms for the following colleges:
>
> (College Names & Code Numbers)
>
> Also enclosed is my check in the amount of $_______. Please send to those schools listed above the SAT results of the test taken on ___________.
>
> Thank you for your courtesy and cooperation.
>
> Sincerely,
>
> Stuart S. Student

They should be able to get those scores to the colleges in about three weeks. Again, put a checkmark in the space on the Flow Chart and follow up, as you did with the transcripts and teacher recommendations, three weeks hence.

The College Board also has a Rush Reporting Service which, for a few extra dollars, will send the test scores to the colleges within two working days after your request is received. You give all the information over the telephone. The number is (212) 966-5853 extension 7600.

Many parents are concerned as to what the scores actually mean. We discussed a little of that aspect earlier in this book but one question persists:

"How do you interpret the College Board scores?"

SAT-Verbal and SAT-Mathematics scores are each reported on a scale of 200 to 800. I refer you to the chart below which details the scores by the student taking the test and alongside it a percentile ranking that compares the results with those seniors who took the test in previous years.

SAT-Verbal Score	***% who did better in previous years***
800	0
750	0.5
700	1.0
650	1.5
600	4.5
550	7.0
500	15.5
450	24.0
400	35.5
350	50.5
300	68.5
250	88.0
200	97.5
SAT-Mathematics	
800	0
750	0.5
700	1.0
650	3.5
600	7.5
550	14.5
500	23.5
450	34.0
400	48.5
350	66.0
300	85.5
250	98.0
200	99.0

Thus, if the score is 500 on the verbal SAT, you will see that 15.5% of the senior boys and girls of previous years did better than your child. Accordingly, the higher score your child achieves will be met with a reduction in the percentage of those who scored better in prior years. A score of 700 on the math test indicates that only 1% of the seniors in years past fared better; in effect, your child exceeded 99% of those previous seniors tested. Conversely, if the score was 200, it is clear that 99% of the students did better than your child.

It should be noted that the tests do not have a passing or failing mark, and they are certainly not scored on a curve, meaning that the results of the scores of other students who took the test with your child had no effect on what your child achieved. The percentile rank simply shows how well your child did compared with students who took the test in the past.

As far as an average is concerned, it was reported last year that the national mean score of all seniors in the verbal test was 414 while in the math it was 457.

A query on retaking the tests. Many parents wonder if the student's score will rise appreciably. It's difficult to make a hard and fast statement about this. Suffice to say, most increases are not that startling, even with a tutor involved. The average increase is about 30 points overall. Approximately one student in 20 gains 100 points or more and approximately one in 100 loses 100 or more points. Students whose first test scores are low usually achieve score gains on retests; however, students whose initial test scores are high don't achieve much more thereafter.

Keep in mind that colleges view different qualities in applicants: College A may be looking for leadership potential while College B may place more emphasis on various extra-curricular activities. College C might have an open admissions policy that admits all applicants no matter what their test scores are while College D might admit students within a certain range only.

Again, follow up to make sure that (1) the test is taken, and (2) the scores are reported to the colleges of your choice as quickly as possible.

As long as we're on the subject of the paperwork involved in the application process, let's hold the question of interviews for a while longer until we've discussed two other areas: one involving the athlete and the other concerning special entry.

Special Entry

What we are primarily talking about is early admission, sometimes called "Quick Action." It doesn't mean that the student starts school ahead of others; it has to do with the acceptance/rejection process. The paperwork is completed well before the deadline for general applications with the intention being that the school will review those early applicants first to determine whether any of them are acceptable. You must specifically request such an early decision. The caveat here is that in return for securing an early acceptance on the application, the student will be obligated to matriculate at the college, if accepted. Needless to say, this has its advantages and disadvantages.

One favorable aspect is the fact that if the student desperately wants to attend that school, forsaking all others, then an early admission acceptance will suit him fine. It'll save time, energy and money. If he's not sure he wants that school but wishes to keep his options open, then early admission may not be best because the student no longer has that option by locking himself into the particular school. Again, this is a personal decision.

Early admission, though, is not for everyone and the principal criterion to determine whether or not your child should make application in that process revolves around his chances of being accepted. You wouldn't exactly want to apply for early admission at M.I.T. with its 1450 SAT average and high grade point average if your child's SAT is 770 and his grade point average is 2.1. For that matter, he shouldn't be applying to M.I.T. anyway—whether early admission or not.

Along with the early admission procedure (which, by the way, not all schools have), there is the special entry qualification. Keep in mind that it's not only the athlete who gets preferential consideration and treatment. There are plenty of others. For example, a top musician might contribute to a school's music program by attending the college and playing in the orchestra over the next four years. In many instances, a college's specific department (in this case, the music department) would work with the admissions office to secure the potential student.

My tactic when it comes to this is to let that department know about the student separately from admissions. In other words, I prepare a resume (sample enclosed) evidencing the student's special talents and I send it to the head of the department. You can get those names from the catalogues. As you can see from the sample, the scheduled major was finance with a music minor.

As a result, a number of schools forwarded materials from the music departments advising of their various programs. For instance, Susquehanna University in Selinsgrove, Pennsylvania, offers a Bachelor of Music in (1) Music Education that prepares the student for music teaching, (2) performance and studio teaching for those who wish to pursue careers as performers or private studio teachers, and (3) church music, providing students with career preparation for teaching and performing in the church.

There was also developed at the college a program combining Music and Business for the student interested in a business career with a music-related company.

Needless to say, like the athlete (who you will read about later on in this chapter), the "special interest group," as I like to call them, outside of admissions could then exert whatever influence it has on persuading admissions to accept the student.

And, as you can see, it isn't limited to extracurricular activities. A student who is the recipient of a national merit honor will be given special treatment right up there with the quarterback of the football team. The key here is to let the proper people know about any such achievements. But, don't simply list them on the application form and feel that will be enough. Let it be known to others outside the admissions office. In other words, a little self-horn-tooting is perfectly acceptable...and desirable. (Incidentally, there are plenty of scholarships and grants for non-athletes and these will be discussed in the subsequent chapter.)

The Student-Athlete

First things first. The definitions. Much has been made of the athlete and the alleged preferential treatment he/she gets. Some people claim that the athlete is the tail wagging the dog; others say it is the dog itself. Whatever the answer, there is no question that the athlete has a hallowed place reserved on most college campuses. More often than we would like to believe, the viability of the entire college may be determined by its athletic program. Pull the plug on a number one football team and the whole school will suffer. Drop the basketball program and watch enrollment decrease. Some colleges have even gone into bankruptcy because a sport was deleted from the program.

And, in the midst of all this strolls your child.

Now, as a high school athlete, your child will be in demand by many colleges, especially if his grades are decent. In some instances, the demand will even cancel out bad grades; sometimes all of them. Thus, if you have a superstar on your hands, then you will be bombarded with inquiries about your child. A number of schools will offer the moon; others chunks of it.

It's all rather flattering...to a certain extent. But remember, the colleges are looking at the athlete like he's a piece of meat. The better the athlete, the better the performance of the team, the better the satisfaction of the alumni, the better the existence of the school. As I said before, the tail wagging the dog, but which is which?

The athlete is a special creature primarily because he/she is dealt with in a different way. Much of that can be created by you. Let's break this down.

Basically, there are two levels of athletes. First, there is the superstar. That is the one who is always written up in the newspapers and to whom the major schools generally flock in droves. There is little you have to do about this athlete.

For example, in most areas there are local scouts for major colleges. They attend high school game after high school game looking for possible players to attend the big college. If they find a good prospect, they'll make the initial contact with the player or player's parents or coach.

So, if your son or daughter is a superstar, chances are you will have the schools running after you with all kinds of enticements. As a result, some of the matters we discussed earlier, such as preparing the many forms, will probably be of little importance to you. With a superstar, the college will bend over backwards to see that the necessary documentation is complete. Of course, with the recent crackdown by the NCAA (National Collegiate Athletic Association) on athletic eligibility, it is still vital that the student have at least a 2.0 grade point average in order to qualify and compete.

What this means is that if your child wants to practice and play his freshmen year at an NCAA Division I or Division II college, he must satisfy the requirements of NCAA Bylaw 14.3, commonly known as Proposition 48. This requires him to graduate from high school, attain a 2.0 GPA in a successfully completed core curriculum of at least 11 academic courses, and achieve a 700 combined score on the SAT or an 18 composite score on the ACT.

If you're the parent of a superstar then, you will have other problems as well. With all these schools running after your child, it becomes a rather heady proposition where one is apt to lose one's perspective. After all, there may be all kinds of inducements thrown at you and the student. But, the bottom line still comes down to one person...the student.

Let's digress for just a moment to explain a point in greater detail. Basically, there are three divisions within the NCAA: I, II & III. For the most part, Division III consists of smaller schools where, under NCAA rules, they are not permitted to give the famed "Athletics Scholarship." They can only assist with financial aid depending on need. Oh sure, there are some short cuts here but these schools are not in the position under the regulations to hand out the renowned four-year full-pay scholarship.

Keep in mind that under the NCAA rules, there is no guaranteed four-year athletics scholarships. An athletics scholarship is awarded for no more than one academic year. It may, however, be renewed each year for a maximum of five years within a six-year period.

There is no question that if you go back over the years, some of the powerhouse colleges in athletics (Alabama, Oklahoma, Georgia, Nebraska, Michigan, Ohio State, Texas, U.S.C., to name a few), were rather loose with their money. A hot-shot ball player would be given a four-year, free ride and, of course, it was not unheard of for the schools to be bidding against each other. Most did. On top of the four year education, one would furnish a car, another would offer money for a job that was in name only, another would supply an apartment, one even bought a house for the parents.

The bidding was fierce and the student-athlete was in the best position to pick and choose whoever would come up with the most exotic offer.

Nobody is saying that this is solely a thing of the past. It still goes on today. But certainly, there has been more awareness of these "gifts" and a number of schools have been placed on probation by the NCAA because of what was deemed bad recruiting tactics. Recently, one midwestern school was cited for playing and paying a top basketball player for four years who, upon graduation, people discovered could neither read nor write above a sixth grade level.

The NCAA has certainly clamped down on these tawdry practices and others similar, like admitting ineligible students. Today, there is a keener understanding by the general public of what may be legitimate and what may not. As someone who was engaged in athletics at college and who had children in athletics, my advice to you is to monitor the activities of these schools rather closely.

When it comes to the superstar, you have an obligation as a parent to see that your child is getting a good education above anything else. It's fine to participate in college sports. I don't have to remind you that the sports pages are always filled with those *few* athletes who go into professional ball and earn megabucks. But, I emphasize the word "few." In proportion to the total number of athletes in colleges throughout the country, those who actually become millionaires are vastly small. There is really only a handful in relation to all athletes.

Don't be deceived. As a result, you have to watch out for certain things with respect to the big-time schools and the superstar.

1) Make sure that it is a school your child really wants. In other words, don't let the enticement of the big bucks determine where he might go. He might discover after the first year that he doesn't want to be in the woods of Arkansas, or he may find that living in the City of Angels is not his idea of heaven. So, be sure that the environment is acceptable to your child., There is no question that a personal visit as well as talks with other students are mandatory.

2) Scrutinize the offer. What does it actually include? The full ride scholarship has pretty much been relegated to the backshelf. Colleges are smarter today. Although they realize there is money in sports, they no longer automatically throw a four year, no-cut scholarship worth in excess of $50,000 at the student indiscriminately. Most schools like to play it one year at a time, in keeping with current NCAA rules. After all, why furnish a full, four year scholarship to a football player who may decide at the end of the first season that he doesn't want to play anymore. What is the college then getting in return for its money during the next three years?

Many colleges have reverted to one year at a time to cover this position. Of course, the question of injury is something else. And that's why it's important to you as the parent to understand completely how the funds are being distributed. Is it intended to apply even if the student is injured? Clarify this point. Also, check to make sure the school is not then on probation. Keep in mind that every athlete likes to be in the limelight. Therefore, a school on probation may be prevented from playing in post-season championship games and on television.

3) Don't grab something now only to find that because of your own greed or ignorance, the student is disallowed from further competition. You have seen and heard countless times about these alumni booster clubs who, on top of the scholarship offer, shower the student with cars, jobs (no work attached), houses, stereos, tickets to games, etc. I can give you only one warning: Watch It! Only accept the offer for tuition, room, board and books.

Each academic year, the student must sign a statement regarding his or her eligibility, recruitment, financial aid and amateur status under NCAA rules. Accordingly, be careful the eligibility is not jeopardized through involvement in violation of NCAA legislation. If there is a work-study program, find out all the particulars. Be careful about taking any cars, houses, apartments, stereos and surely, no money. The temptation is great but there are too many athletes who have ruined their careers because of greed.

If in doubt as to the legitimacy of any offer, feel free to contact the NCAA at 6201 College Boulevard Overland Park, Kansas 66211-2422. Telephone (913) 339-1906. The executive director is Richard D. Schultz. They would be more than happy to guide you. There is also a pamphlet distributed by the NCAA that is quite valuable. It's entitled *"NCAA Guide for the College-Bound Student-Athlete"* and it's free for the asking.

What if your child is not a superstar but is a decent athlete? For the most part, he may not have all the big schools running after him, or he may have a minimum number of colleges sitting on his doorstep. Generally, I have taken a different tact here, one that I have used quite successfully with my own children and with many other student-athletes.

Again, there's a little work cut out for you but I can practically guarantee that the rewards at the end of the road will be more than worth it.

First of all, I prepare a short bio of the student. As you can see in the sample enclosed, I list as many things as possible, and not only athletic. Actually, I start with the personal and academic areas which pave the way for the sports.

Secondly, I go to the Grey Book. This is a book that is published by the NCAA. It is generally not found in any library or bookstore and if you talk with the coach in your school, or contact the NCAA, you should be able to obtain a copy. The book lists all the colleges in the U.S. with a breakdown of what sports are played there on the intercollegiate level and what scholarships or other monies are offered in what sports. It is akin to B*arron's* book on finding colleges but here the emphasis is on athletics.

Armed with your child's Profile as to what kind of college he seeks, and with the materials gleaned from the Grey Book, I then send a form letter to each athletic director (notice not the coach of the particular sport but rather the Director of Athletics), enclosing the bio and asking for application forms and other materials. The letter comes from your child, and it's a rather simple form:

> Dear ____________________:
>
> I will be graduating from high school next June and would be interested in your college program.
>
> Enclosed is a resume of my accomplishments to date.
>
> My main concern is making sure that I am in a school that will afford me a solid atmosphere for my chosen major coupled with realistic athletic participation.
>
> If interested, would you kindly send me the necessary application materials.

Now, you will note a few things about this letter. One, you are letting the college know that the student is in school first for an education. Secondly, you want them to review the resume and understand that the student wants to couple the education with "realistic athletic participation." In effect, you're saying to the athletic director, "Look, here's what I've done so far. I'm not interested in simply sitting on the bench for four years. I want to participate. Based upon what you see in this resume, is yours the school for me?"

In one example, the form letter was sent to some 73 schools. That's right, 73. Oh, not all of them conformed to the Profile. We went to a few outside the area just to see what they would say.

Of those 73 schools, we received 62 responses, meaning that materials and special athletic forms from 62 colleges were sent us. That, to me, represented a darn good turnout. All of the materials were accompanied by appropriate letters from the appropriate coaches. It was rather satisfying.

But, of the 62 responses, we discounted at least half of them right off the bat. One college was interested if the boy made it to the State wrestling final; that sounded like a pressure school. Another was interested but we discovered it was in the middle of North Dakota with only prairie brush around. "No go," said the athlete.

Another was hedgy on whether the student could participate although they would "certainly look at him." What did that mean?

One was placed on probation a day later. We quickly discarded those. Another advised us that all athletic scholarships had been given out for the year (already?) but that the student could try out for the team as a walk-on. Really? Forget them.

There is one other fascinating aspect that must be considered here. You will find that when application forms are sent as a result of an athletic interest, they will probably be specially coded. One college coach sent this letter:

> "You have been recommended to me as a wrestling candidate. Please fill out and return the enclosed information sheet so that I will have the necessary information to assist you.It is very advantageous for you to apply early and use only the 'specially marked' application that I will send you. Please do not use an unmarked application."

Don't you love it? In effect, the athletic department is deciding what they want or how much leeway they are permitting the admissions people. They expect to be able to exert enough pressure to have the candidate accepted. One college coach told me this outright: "We get what we want."

Now, what's your position? If they want a certain application form filled out, that is not your problem. You just make sure there is nothing illegal being peddled, like a form that talks about how much money the student will get, or how many cars, etc. Just keep in mind that neither the parent nor the student may receive any benefit, inducement or arrangement such as cash, clothing, cars, improper expenses, transportation, gifts or loans to encourage the signing of any letter of intent or to attend an NCAA school.

I do have one amusing story here showing what sometimes happens between the right hand and the left, one being the admissions office and the other being the athletic department.

We had an incident with a major, well-respected, top-ranked college situated in the midwest. Now, I am not talking about an athletics factory. I'm referring to a university that has an extraordinary reputation, and primarily good.

The school was interested in this boy for baseball. Fine. The student received an application, completed it and returned it to the admissions office. The application indeed did have a "B" code on it that apparently meant Baseball.

A while later, the parent received an inquiry from the coach. The papers were all being filed but where was the application form?

"The application form," the parent explained to the coach over the telephone, "was sent in weeks ago."

"Weeks ago? I should have received it."

"Well, why not ask admissions? They must have it by now."

There was a gasp on the other end.

"Admissions? What's it doing with them?"

There was a pause.

"Why not? Where else was I to send it?"

Another gasp.

"Oh no, you never should have sent it to them. It should have come back to me. Now we've got problems."

Would you believe this conversation? Subsequently, the parent learned that the admissions office and the athletic department were handling admissions on a separate basis. In other words, if the form was sent directly to admissions, then the athletic people had no "power of persuasion" over admissions and could only cross their fingers hoping that the administration would accept the student. Needless to say, this is a school that receives many more applicants than it has available places. However, if the application form was returned to the athletics people, then they could "walk the form over to admissions" and be assured they would get an acceptance.

There was only one question in the parent's mind when he heard this: "Aren't you all one university?"

No response.

Now, going back to the case at hand, we were finally left with some 31 schools and then we whittled that down to 16. I thought it was the N.I.T.

I suggested something else which, although costly, paid for itself many times over. Inasmuch as the student participated in a high-profile sport, I suggested films be made of the best outings. It cost $194.50 to put together and duplicate three films that had been taken by the high school's athletic department. These were then bicycled around to the remaining schools on the list. I wanted to make sure that I wasn't overestimating a college and what better way then to let them see for themselves what the kid actually looked like participating in the actual sport.

It worked. We were able to weed out another 6 schools whose interest was marginal at best and we thus applied to the 10 schools who really had an interest and who were in tune with the Profile.

I have used this system with students of many other friends and relatives...all with success.

Incidentally, there is one final aspect here and if you recognize my pattern you may quickly see what it is: Thank you notes. Definitely make sure that the coaches of your child's high school teams are fully aware of what schools you are applying to, for many times the college coach will contact the high school for reference. In addition, a little thank you note for past and future cooperation wouldn't hurt either.

The Personal Interview

The final piece of paperwork before you head into the financial arena doesn't really have to do with paper. Rather, it concerns the student's interview. As I mentioned before, I feel it is important that there be an interview at each college of choice. You will note from the various application paraphernalia that many colleges say the personal interview is not mandatory and is not even essential to the admissions procedure. That may be so but to me, it cuts two ways.

If you have a recluse for a child or one who is extraordinarily shy, it would be a disaster to expose him to a potentially stressful interview. Accordingly, it might be best to sidestep this. However, these children aren't bad on interviews at all. In fact, the student does fairly well; the parents are the basket cases.

I suggest that you request an interview from someone from admissions. This enables you to look at the school in the event you haven't seen it as yet and it gives you an opportunity to talk with some of the administration. The latter is a good barometer of the college itself.

Most of us view the "grilling"of the student as the final test to see if the college will accept him. Hogwash! I take the opposite view. I am interested in how the college stacks up. After all, I consider that my money (and hopefully it is the college's) is good anywhere and therefore, I take a rather cavalier attitude toward spending it. In any event, I suggest that you ask for the interview in writing (you want that as part of the file, too) and don't forget to have it confirmed. Most colleges will try to dovetail the interview with a tour of the campus and many will accommodate working parents by conducting same on a weekend, primarily Saturday. In this respect, parents can accompany the student, have a guided tour of the campus and be able to see exactly what kind of people the college employs. A well-run admissions office is indicative of the school. Incidentally, many recent graduates are used in admissions, either as tour guides, clerks or assistants; some even as interviewers.

Now, as to dress code, I am one of those who don't believe in gilding the lily. Too often, I see prospective students waltzing into the interview room looking as though they were ready to step out in the Easter Parade. Some appear to have been dressed by Vogue magazine while others are wearing the latest fashion in the area, no matter what it looks like.

At this stage, let me talk directly to the student:

Keep in mind that there is an enormous bridge between high school and college, and the Betty Boop sweatshirt that was so popular in the hallways of Forest Hills High will look quite out of place among the ivy-covered buildings Princeton University. The best bet is to wear rather conservative clothes and to make sure they don't look like they have just been bought for the occasion. Thus, if you have a new pair of shoes, wear them a couple of times. One admissions officer told me she felt disconcerted by having to sit across from soles that looked like they hadn't even touched the ground yet. She thought the student must have put them on in the waiting room for the first time. This was much too obvious.

For you males, you can't really go wrong with a button-down plaid or striped shirt, grey slacks and the perennial blue blazer. There is no need for a tie. Sneaks are verboten; penny loafers are perfectly fine. You must look comfortable, yet well-dressed and relaxed. This is not your confirmation, or wedding.

Needless to say, you should look well-groomed. Your hair shouldn't be down to your navel and your fingernails (a most important part) should be clean. And, you should have a fresh shave unless, of course, you sport a beard; that should be trimmed. Nothing scraggly. Again, the intent is to look clean.

For you females, forget the sweatshirts and jeans with high heels. You're not going to a disco or club, and the admissions officer will not be impressed with your attempt to show what's "in." Keep it simple with a dress and low-heeled shoes (remember, you may have to hike around the campus on the guided tour and you don't want to limp from building to building). You should wear a conservative dress, or sweater and skirt. This is *not* the place for a suit with blouse and tie. You're not in the corporate headquarters of General Motors. And, by the same token, don't come strolling in with gobs of makeup and swinging a sequined handbag. You are not ambling up the avenue to the local sweetshop to meet a date. In addition, go easy with any fancy hairdo and nailpolish. Simple, clean and unobtrusive is your best bet.

Don't forget that you will probably be interviewed by a rather youngish admissions counselor, perhaps only a few years out of school himself. He will most likely be conservatively dressed and will be serious about what he is doing. To be sure, this is a serious matter. An interview can sometimes make the difference between acceptance and rejection. Although most colleges claim it is not the major criterion in deciding whether an applicant will be accepted or not, it is still an important element and could sway a doubtful decision one way or the other.

You must also be there on time. There is just no excuse for lateness. Most interviews are scheduled with a number of others so that if you are late, you could easily throw the entire schedule off. That's not exactly the best way to make friends and influence people. You must be prompt.

It's always easy to get sidetracked when coming onto a campus for the first time. Many parents advise that they are fascinated by their surroundings instead of concentrating on getting to the admissions office. I suggest that you fix your eyes straight ahead and get yourself first to the admissions office before you stop to watch the soccer team practice on the beautiful green field beside the lake where people are feeding swans. You can do all that later.

Now, for you parents, here comes the shocker. The interview is with your child, the student, and not you. So, if you are gearing yourself up for your own presentation, put it on the back burner. You will be met by the admissions people and, therefore, you too should be decently dressed and groomed, but the body of the interview will take place out of your earshot and eyesight between the admissions counselor and the student. Remember, the student is the one enrolling there, not you...as difficult as that must be to swallow.

You will be brought into the picture at the end. The admissions people like to see the interaction between the parents and the student. Thus, if you have been arguing with your spouse or even with the child, make sure you have left that argument on the doorstep. You want to show harmony. You are there to aid in the child's acceptance. For you divorced couples, the sign is apparent: leave those ill-feelings in your respective cars. *Don't let the child suffer!*

Preparing the student is important. He must be familiar with the application that was filed in the event he's questioned about it and he should know something of the school itself. Quizzing him on the school's history and its various courses of study is important. He should also have a few questions prepared but not those readily available in the literature. No admissions person likes to hear, "So, when was the school founded?"

What they do like to hear are these questions:

1) What's the faculty/student ratio in my chosen major? In other words, how many students are there to one teacher?

2) How many PhD's are there? This will indicate the possible quality of the teaching. Good teachers like to flock to good schools.

3) What's the percentage of returning freshmen? Translated, how many come back for the second year? The number says something about the school. A high percentage is 90+, while a low is 50.

4) From where are most of the undergraduates? It's nice to have a cross-section of the country rather than everybody from one closely-defined area.

5) Are there any major contributors to the school? This is important to know because it may affect career placement. For example, Marist College in Poughkeepsie, New York, is known affectionately as "The IBM Connection," because many of the students in the computer field go to IBM after graduation.

You can find questions pertaining to other majors, as well. For instance, what percentage of the pre-med students get accepted to medical school and which schools? You can zero-in on almost any major to see how well the graduates do.

6) Do you have a job placement service? Some aid in getting student employment. By the same token, a flip side question is, do many companies recruit from this campus. You're trying to ascertain whether firms send people to the college looking for future employees.

As I said before, usually the student will be taken to another room for the interview. The parents do join the conversation but much later. No two schools function alike but based upon the interviewers I have spoken to, here is what they look for first:

A) They check the student's physical appearance. That's why it's important to look decent.

B) They watch general composure. Of course, they realize how nervous the student might be and they can compensate for the one who is sitting ramrod straight in the chair, hands clasped. That, they consider, is perfectly normal. But what they don't particularly like is the student who is slumped halfway off the seat. Boys are notorious in doing this.

C) No smoking, even if the interviewer does. And no gum chewing, eating a tunafish sandwich or chomping on a chocolate bar. It sounds silly to suggest that this is done but one admissions person told me of the student who rushed into the interview clutching a paperbag filled with a hamburger, french fries and soft drink. She explained that she didn't have time for lunch because "My hair didn't dry on time and then I got this call from my girl friend who..."

It goes without saying that the interviewer is not interested in the student's personal life to this extent and is certainly not thrilled about the student having lunch on his time.

For the most part, the interviewer will try and make every effort to relax the student. It doesn't always work this way and some interviewers are admittedly terrible at it. They might even be perusing the file as though they were seeing it for the first time. It could be. When it comes to admissions, the decision on acceptance or rejection is generally a group one. There may be two persons assigned to your child: one to review the paperwork and another just to conduct the interview. Thus, when the full admissions body meets, each person puts in her own opinion of you and the group then votes as a whole. So, you might very well be encountering an admissions person who is unfamiliar with the application form, the transcript, SAT scores, etc. In fact, sometimes they have never even seen that documentation and are simply talking to the student without any knowledge as to the backup material.

As to the questions that are asked of the student, this runs the gamut. They are, however, designed to extract information. Here are a few samples for the student to bear in mind:

Question: How did you get interested in the college?

Response: I would tell the truth. If through a friend, mention the name. If through your parents, say so. The college is vitally interested in how their name got to your ears.

Question: Why do you want to come to our college?

Response: Here you may have to polish the apple a bit. Most schools have similar courses, so the claim that "I want to come here because this school has the best program for abnormal sexuality" may not hold water. Of course, if it's M.I.T. and your answer is "I want to attend M.I.T. because it's considered the top engineering school in the country," you may get no argument from most quarters.

Question: What did you do in high school?

Response: This sounds like a loaded question or a stupid one and at first blush you may want to suggest that the interviewer look at your file, but there is a reason behind the query. The interviewer may not have reviewed your file and wants to hear about your high school career from your lips, or the interviewer has seen the file but still wants to hear about it from your own lips. This is especially true when you list awards on the application form in, for example, debating but you can't seem to get out one whole sentence on the interview without stuttering. Therefore, it would be advantageous to review the application form before you go into the interview. That's why it's so important to keep a photocopy of it on hand.

Question: What are your plans for the future?

Response: Don't try and con your way through the question. It won't work. If you're clear as to where you are heading, then expound on that. If you're unsure, then say so. You won't be faulted for being undecided; that's some of what college is supposed to clarify, to make you more aware of what options are indeed open.

Question: Are your parents pleased with your selection of this college?

Response: This affords the interviewer an opportunity to discuss this aspect with the parents in the event of disagreement.

Many interviewers, after the basic questioning, will shift the focus away from school in order to discuss a number of different topics simply to get the student into a free-wheeling, unstructured environment. The intention here is to see what is below the programmed surface. The interviewers like to see someone who has ideas. I would recommend that a week before the interview you read one of the weekly newsmagazines to bring you up to date on current events. Incidentally, try not to get too political but do say what's on your mind. Just make sure it's with some thought. It doesn't help to engage in a conversation like this:

Interviewer: "You don't like politics?"
Student: "Not really."
Interviewer: "Why?"
Student: "I don't know."
Interviewer: "What about the Mayor. She's done a lot, hasn't she?"
Student: "I don't care for her."
Interviewer: "Why?"
Student: "I don't know."

And, this is a true story. So, if you are going to make a statement, be sure you know something about it. Check the facts. Don't just talk to hear your voice. And, don't be afraid to ask questions of the interviewer. Everybody likes to talk about themselves and the interviewer is no exception. Ask questions about him too. In other words, don't sit there like a bump on a log trying to field question upon question. Engage in a give-and-take conversation. That's the most important aspect of all.

Finally, don't forget to send a thank you note to the interviewer, letting him know that he should contact you if any additional information is required. And, reaffirm your interest in the school if, in fact, you're still interested after the day is done.

The last item in this chapter is a simple one. Check with the colleges periodically to see if the file is complete. Keep tabs on the Flow Chart; that's the key to it all.

Now, let's get into the next main section, **Money**...and where to find it.

Chapter 3

PAYING FOR COLLEGE

It is said that the best things in life are free. That may be true to some limited—very limited—extent, but when it comes to college, it has no standing. Finding money for college is one of the most nerve-wrenching aspects of this entire matter; to say it is a necessary evil would indeed be an understatement.

However, before you step off blindly into the labyrinth of the area known as "Financial Aid," you should not forget that unless your name is Rockefeller, there really and truly are funds available to you in different forms to help pay for this schooling. In fact, more than $26 billion was available last year alone to aid students with the Federal Student Aid plan providing some 75% of the total aid. That's one of the reasons why I don't believe in ruling out any particular school based solely on its costs. Many people have placed their children in fancy, private schools and paid less than if the student had enrolled in a state school. Money is definitely available but what you must know is where the sources are and when to tap them.

When we talk about financial aid, we are referring to those funds needed to meet all college costs: tuition, fees, room and board (if applicable), books, even transportation. You should also understand that financial aid comes in three forms and you can get it all from either one source or from any combination. They are:

Grants/Scholarships: These are sometimes called "gifts." They are awards based upon certain criteria such as academic achievement or need, and do not have to be repaid.

Loans: These come from lending institutions and, of course, do have to be repaid but usually after the student finishes college and at an extremely low interest rate, not to mention on extraordinarily favorable repayment terms.

Employment: This covers the student being employed part-time at the college. It's sometimes called the Work-Study Program.

Now, before we begin on the road to securing such aid in any of the above forms, or all of them, I must re-emphasize the fact that no student should shy away from applying for money simply because he "thinks" he won't qualify. Last year, more than three million students—that's right, three million—received aid. And, you don't have to be destitute to evidence financial need. "Need," by the way, is considered the difference between what it costs to attend a particular college and what you and the student can afford to pay toward those costs. Keep in mind that students usually are eligible for financial aid equal to the amount of their demonstrated financial need. Inasmuch as the amount a family can afford to pay stays pretty much the same, whether the costs of the college are high or low, it is easily seen that the student would be eligible for varying amounts of aid at various colleges.

Try this on for size. The prestigious Princeton University notes that more than 40% of its undergraduates receive financial aid and that last year alone the University awarded more than $23 million in financial aids to undergraduates. Yes, you read it right. $23 million. According to the University, "Princeton has traditionally met the demonstrated financial need of everyone offered admission, and expects to continue that policy in the future."

And that's not an aberration.

Go from Princeton to the smaller Lynchburg College. Of the 47% who applied for financial aid last year, some 72% of those were judged to have need and 99% of those were given aid. And at Susquehanna University, 415 of 500 were judged to need financial aid with an average aid award of $10,172.

I remind you once again that if you receive all the financial aid you are eligible for, you could conceivably end up paying the same amount at a high-cost college as you would at a lower-cost one. It's happened to me and many others.

Let's talk briefly about what is generally available. You will readily see the width of this spectrum:

Types of Aid

Scholarships/Grants: Don't poo-poo this in any way. You would be pleasantly surprised at what is available if you just do a little digging beneath the surface.

A "grant" is an outright gift of money from a particular fund. For example, a school may have "X" dollars available to give to qualified students as part of its financial aid program. They call the awards "grants" and they are generally earmarked for a specific purpose: academic achievement, athletic achievement, financial need, etc.

Depending on the school, there are, for the most part, three categories of scholarships: need-based "Special Scholarships" and the competitive "Honor Scholarships" and "Athletic Scholarships."

In order to receive one of the need-based "Special Scholarships," the student must have academic merit and must show financial need for such an award. (Incidentally, when need is involved, you must file the FAF or Financial Aid Form, which we will discuss in depth in the next section.)

What you must do is review carefully the individual college's catalogue under "Financial Aid" to ascertain what sorts of scholarships/grants are available. They are varied. In many instances, donors have placed funds in the school's coffers with certain requirements attached as to who should receive what awards. For example, at Lynchburg College in Lynchburg, Virginia, there are a number of different scholarships available such as (1) the T. Brady Saunders Award (amounts to $3,000) which is given to students in the top 10% of the high school class with an SAT score of at least 1000, (2) the Disciples Merit Award (worth $1,000) given to members of the Christian Church with a strong academic and church record, (3) a $1,000 grant called the Baptist Nursing Honor awarded to nursing majors who are members of the Baptist Church, and (4) The Central Virginia Black Teachers Scholarship given to black high school seniors from local public high schools who are planning careers in public school teaching. And Lynchburg has many more.

Look at Swarthmore College, in Swarthmore, Pennsylvania, just outside Philadelphia. For the academic year 1990-91, the College awarded $6 million in grants, with one-half of that sum provided through special gifts and endowed scholarships. In its financial aid brochure, the College lists a mind-boggling 9 pages of scholarships. These are just a few samples to show you the range, but each college's catalogue will list in detail a myriad of special grants to which the student may apply.The interesting aspect is that many students *never* apply for such monies and many of these awards lie dormant from year to year.

Recipients in the "Honor & Athletic Scholarships" category are selected on the basis of academic or athletic merit without having to document financial need. Again, many of these go unrequested, strange as it seems.

You are also encouraged to check with your high school to see if the student qualifies for any of the scholarships offered by local clubs or community agencies.

You could check too with your own state which generally provides grants for scholarships for residents. Here are a few examples: In Virginia, the Tuition Assistance Grant Program is available to Virginia residents attending private colleges in that state; in Connecticut, the state's Undergraduate Scholarship Program is a need-based aid program for residents of Connecticut; in Pennsylvania, the State Scholarship Program provides a need-based assistance for its residents while in New York State, there is a new Liberty Scholarship for 1991-92 and a Tuition Assistance Program which is a grant arrangement for New York residents attending colleges within the state. Undergraduate students are eligible for up to four years of aid for full-time study or up to five years in certain programs.

Some states have broader coverages. The Vermont Student Assistance Corporation provides incentive grants for its residents who attend specific out-of-state colleges while in New York, there is even a $1,100 award to members of Indian tribes.

What you must do is contact the colleges for a full explanation of their various financial aid programs and I would add the Higher Education Services Department, or Department of Education, in your own state. In many areas, there are a slew of scholarships, fellowships and other awards available ranging from a grant of money to children of police officers or firefighters, to a scholarship for children of veterans who served in the U.S. armed forces. One need only to look to find considerable funds available.

The most well-known of the grants is the Pell Grant administered by the federal government. The program is designed to provide financial assistance to students with heavy financial need. Eligibility is determined by the government as a result of the financial data submitted by the student and his family. Best of all, these monies do *not* need to be repaid.

The federal government also provides assistance known as SEOG, the Supplemental Educational Opportunity Grant, to students demonstrating need. Again, they are not repaid.

Loans: The Perkins Student Loan (formerly The National Direct Student Loan [NDSL]) is a program sponsored by the government that provides for the awarding of loans averaging $2,250 per year to students who evidence lack of financial support for college. Loans are usually made by a combination of monies received from the federal government and matched by the colleges, as well as funds repaid by previous borrowers.

The amounts are determined by the college within federal limits. There is no interest charged during school and for a number of months afterwards, or during military service. The interest is 5% on the unpaid balance and students are required to start repaying the loan beginning nine months after they graduate or leave school. The repayment can take up to ten years. Actually, students going on to graduate school are even eligible to defer payment while in the graduate program.

The Robert T. Stafford Student Loan (formerly called the Guaranteed Student Loan) is a form of student financial aid which is administered through the student's hometown bank and state loan authorities. The loans are low-interest (8%) and need not be repaid until after the student graduates or leaves college and, again, under favorable terms; the minimum monthly payment is only $50. As with Perkins, the repayment may be deferred while the student is attending graduate school or is in the armed forces, peace corps or comparable service.

There are also other interesting loan arrangements such as the one set up by the Omnibus Budget Reconciliation Act of 1981 which expanded the scope of the Parents Loan Program whereby parents can now borrow certain amounts with the interest rate set at 12%. Repayment begins 60 days after the loan disbursement.

In addition, there are auxiliary loans to assist students, where you only make interest payments while in school. They are generally 12%. Repayment of the amount borrowed begins when the student leaves school.

Depending on your state, there are many other loan arrangements available. For example, New York State has loans for Health Profession Students covering those enrolled in graduate programs of medicine, dentistry, optometry, veterinary medicine, podiatry, or pharmacy. The interest rate is 12% and repayment begins six months after the student leaves graduate school.

Student Employment: The Federal College Work Study Program (CWSP)) offers job opportunities to students who show need. This program makes campus jobs available to students on a part-time basis. It works quite well. My kids had such jobs and they earned some $1500 each a year for part-time work such as a cashier in the bookstore, helping in the snack bar, or secretarial services in the administrative offices. A typical job involves about 12 hours of work per week.

Again, financial aid is readily available. Don't think otherwise.

Colleges will send you a separate booklet or sheet relating to financial aid. I suggest that you review the materials first to see what areas actually apply and to cross off those where you would have no chance whatsoever of picking up money. But, by the same token, you may note that under Grants/State, there is an "other" category, referring to some money which is "variable according to the state in which you reside." That's the reason I suggest you check with your own state's Department of Education to determine whether there are additional grants which would apply.

Most of the other categories are self-explanatory and you should be able to target the appropriate area for financial aid based upon the information supplied by both the college and the state.

As you can see, the most recurring and important one relates to the Financial Aid Form (FAF), which is where the bulk of the grants come into play. When it comes to money, the FAF is the most essential document of all and the one which you MUST complete...and on time.

Let's go into that now.

Financial Aid Form

First of all, where can you get this monster? Primarily from two sources: one is the high school guidance office and the other is the College Scholarship Service (CSS). You are looking for a booklet that says, "FAF/Financial Aid Form" and which is published by the College Scholarship Service of the College Board. However, make sure it is the year you need. If your child is starting college in September of 1992, you want the booklet that is headed "School Year 1992-93" because the aid you are requesting is for the full school year which starts in September of one year and ends in June of the next.

If your high school does not have a copy of the booklet, then call or write the CSS. For those living somewhat east of the Mississippi, meaning the states of Alabama, Connecticut, Delaware, the District of Columbia, Florida, Georgia, Indiana, Kentucky, Louisiana, Maine, Maryland, Massachusetts, Michigan, Mississippi, New Hampshire, New Jersey, New York, North Carolina, Ohio, Pennsylvania, Rhode Island, South Carolina, Tennessee, Vermont, Virginia, West Virginia and Wisconsin, plus Canada, Puerto Rico and the U.S. Virgin Islands, you would write to the College Scholarship Service, CN 6300, Princeton, New Jersey 08541.

If you live in Alaska, American Samoa, Arizona, Arkansas, California, Colorado, Guam, Hawaii, Idaho, Illinois, Iowa, Kansas, Mexico, Minnesota, Missouri, Montana, Nebraska, Nevada, New Mexico, North Dakota, Northern Mariana Islands, Oklahoma, Oregon, South Dakota, Texas, Utah, Washington or Wyoming, you would write to the College Scholarship Service at Box 380, Berkeley, California 94701.

Or, you can call them at a toll-free number: 1-800-772-3537.

You should obtain the FAF around November or December of the student's senior year. You file it on or after January 1st; *not before.*

Now, while you are waiting for the form to arrive, I suggest that you prepare a draft of your tax return for the current year. That's right. As strange and as onerous as it sounds, you will have to know the numbers in your tax return in order to prepare the FAF. I realize that I may be talking about estimating the numbers on the return but there is no choice. For those of you who wait until the last moment to file your income tax return, you will have to change that habit. You must have the FAF filed considerably earlier...preferably as soon after the first of the year as possible. The reason is that the CSS must have sufficient time to analyze the information (which takes about four weeks) before it can send same to the colleges designated by you to receive the results of such analysis.

The college needs time as well in order to prepare a financial aid package prior to the admissions deadline which is usually May 1st. That's when all accepted students must decide whether or not they are going to that college.

Remember, what you are trying to do is to get in with your request as close as feasible to the front of the line. Some schools dole out financial aid on a first-come, first-served basis. Therefore, you can ill-afford to wait until the last minute when their money supply may be exhausted. Also, in the event some additional information is required, you are giving yourself some flexibility—time-wise—to fill that request.

The purpose of the FAF is so the CSS can estimate what you can pay toward the costs of education. Keep in mind that it is only an estimate and the individual colleges make the final decision on how they will grant financial aid. This can be higher or lower than the estimated figure from CSS.

The FAF, by the way, is set up in such a way that by checking certain boxes (as I will indicate), various federal and state agencies dispensing grants will automatically receive a copy of the work done by CSS.

The form is enclosed in the center of the booklet you receive from CSS. Take it out, make a photocopy, and put the original aside. Like we did with the application forms, you want to do a draft first in pencil, so that numbers can be easily erased. The original will require completion by pen. No typewriter here. Also, have the tax information right with you.

You will note that the FAF is set up numerically and there are four pages to complete. Actually, it is the student who should be filling out this form and the words "you" and "your," as used, mean the student. But, as I said before, two good heads are better than one, so work together. This form is too important not to give it your best efforts.

Now, let's start out. The sample here is the one used in New York State, although the form in your area will be primarily the same except for changes to conform with whatever assistance programs apply in your state. The following numbered paragraphs correspond to the numbers in the form. Boxes are answered with an "X" in the appropriate spaces. Turn to Page 1:

Section A.

1. Fill in the student's last name, first name and middle initial. Make sure whatever you do that it is legible and do not write in the margins. Only one letter or number per space.

So far, so good, eh?

2. The address goes here. Skip a space between numbers and letters. For example, if you live at 10 Apple Street, then there should be a blank space between "10" and "Apple" and between "Apple" and "Strcct."
3. Check the appropriate box.
4. The state of legal residence. Obviously, this means where the student actually resides. Abbreviations for the states are on page 2 of the booklet.
5. Social security number. By now, the student should know it by heart.
6. Date of birth. All blanks are filled in. If your daughter was born in August, then the first two spaces over the word "Month" should look like this: 08. If her day of birth is the first, then those spaces should be: 01.
7. Self-explanatory. Simply check the appropriate box. Remember, it's an "X" mark in the box.
8. This is also self-explanatory. Ninety (90%) percent of the time, the first box will be checked.
9. Most of you are dealing with first year students, or incoming freshmen. Thus, you would be checking box 1 here. Of course, if that is not the case, then simply check the applicable box.
10. If your answer to 9 is to check box 1, then the student won't have the bachelor's degree by the following year. Therefore, your answer here would be a "No."

Section B. For the majority of you out there as students, you will be inserting a string of "No's" here. As a result, you will be skipping questions **12-15**. This brings you down to **Section C** where you complete both sides, representing questions **16-21**.

16-21: This is rather easy to do. Keep one thing in mind. The family members referred to here *include* the student. So that if the family includes a mother, father, the student and the student's brother, the total number would be 4. If the student and her brother are both in college, then that number in **19** would be 2.

The first page is now history.

Page 2/Section D: We are preparing to get into the thick of it. Money is now on the table. The first thing you must check is whether the FAF is being completed via a completed tax return or an estimated one, or in a situation where no return will be filed. Check the appropriate box in **22**.

Your (the parent's) tax return, if applicable, should be close at hand for you will be referring to the numbers constantly. Inasmuch as the IRS forms change from year-to-year, it would be best to wait until you have the new income tax return to determine what lines refer to what lines. In other words, the FAF form will refer to a particular line in the IRS form; however, the latter alters its format each year and thus, you must dovetail them. That's why it's important to do your taxes first on the new tax form and bring that to the table when you do the FAF form.

You will also note that there is a corresponding set of boxes (**22** through **28**) relating to the student's income. You would follow the same procedure as you did with your own lines **22-28**.

23. Insert the total number of exemptions from the IRS form.

24. Insert the total income, again from the IRS form.

25. Insert the total of U.S. income tax paid...from the IRS form, of course.

26-27. This breaks down the income from both father and mother. It especially comes into play in divorced situations when the CSS tries to estimate what financial need there may be depending on what each parent may be able to contribute.

28. Here again, the subjects are self-explanatory. You will see in subsection c that there is a place for the amount of child support received.

Section E. Most of you will skip this section, unless you have outstanding government loans.

Section F. Insert the names of three colleges that are highest up on your list. I know there may be more, but take the top three. You'll be able to add to that later.

35. The questions here are whether you want the information from the FAF sent to the financial aid agencies in your state, etc. Without further ado, I suggest you check "Yes" in all boxes. You want as wide a distribution of this material as possible. It can only inure to your benefit. If you don't qualify, so be it. But at least you must make every effort and get the information to all parties concerned with financial aid. Check the boxes in the affirmative.

36. Self-explanatory. For most of you, the box to be checked will be 4.

37. In order to receive federal student aid, you must be registered with Selective Service is you are a male who is at least 18 years old and born after December 31, 1959. Accordingly, you mark this box only if you are 18 through 25 years of age *and* have not registered *and* give Selective Service permission to register you.

38. Signatures by everybody concerned. Don't miss this. If you fail to sign, the form will be returned to you *unprocessed.* That creates all sorts of unwelcome delays.

Section G. We now arrive at various additional numbers relating to medical and dental expenses not paid by insurance. This is important stuff for it tells the CSS what has been coming out of your pocket without reimbursement. They want a number here of all those medical expenses which were not reimbursed by the insurance company. You can refer back to the itemized list of deductions on your tax return or if they weren't itemized, from your own checkbook as to what you paid out without any insurance coverage.

The same applies to tuitions that may have been paid for any others in the family. We're talking about the amount of money that was paid for tuition for others: the parents, children (except the one applying for financial aid), and the like. For example, if there is another child in the family who goes to a private school and tuition was paid for that schooling, it would be included in this section. All these payments show additional expenditures that bolster the need for financial aid. Keep in mind that this area, as the one before, applies to both the parents and the student.

Section H. Displaced? Granted, this is a strange word here. What the CSS is trying to find out when it comes to the assets of both the parents and student is whether or not a person is now unemployed and having trouble finding work, or is on public assistance or works in the home providing unpaid services for family members. It's a way to show the CSS what difficulties presently exist in a family's financial picture.

41. Self-explanatory.

42-47. Include here how much you've got: cash, savings and checking accounts...and only that! The same holds true for the student, as you can see.

If you own a home, you'll have to evaluate it and insert a figure. If you rent, simply write in "0" and go on to the next section.

In addition, the CSS wants to know what other investments you have: stocks, mutual funds, junk bonds, and the like. In other words, if you have $200,000 worth of investments and only $2,000 in your savings account, that won't look as good as $20,000 in the savings account and $900 in investments. For some reason, the CSS people seem to think that investments are a big item. It's akin to the company president who says,"Well on paper I'm worth three zillion dollars but I only have thirty-eight dollars in my pocket; therefore, I don't see how I can pick up this tab for lunch." Huh?

Business and farm assets also go here. Again, the CSS is looking for the worth of such items.

Section I. For 90% of you students, this section won't apply.

Section J. The CSS wants the parent to estimate what the earnings will be next year. Fun, eh? They're trying to see whether or not you should be getting any aid if you expect that your salary will be jumping from its present $40,000 a year to $240,000. (It should happen to all of us.) Again, you refer to the tax return. The numbers are all in there. Needless to say, all you can really do is estimate but, if anything, keep it either the same or on the down side. It certainly won't do you any good to tell the CSS that your income is *definitely* going to triple next year...unless you know for sure.

In addition, what if you are under a contract with an employer and that contract will expire at the end of the year and you either are not being renewed or are not sure? You want to include that information here: "Joe Jones' current contract with the present employer ends on December 31. Renewal of the contract is not expected for next year."

Note that there is a corresponding section referring to the student.

Section K. This is additional information about the student. It's self-explanatory. You might want to take another look at number **61** dealing with your course of study. The instruction booklet, on page 7, has a list of code numbers referring to different courses of study. If you know for sure what it is to be, then insert the number. Otherwise, you can use a "29," which means "Other/ Undecided."

Also, take a gander at **64** and **65**. In the first part, you want to have financial aid cover the full school year. Therefore, if the term begins in September, you may need to have the money in your pocket before then. Accordingly, you may wish to insert a July or August date as the start to ensure that you will have funds in time to pay tuition.

As to the second question, you might want to consider number 2 which covers both bases: part-time job and loan. In other words, don't limit yourself up front. Take as wide a berth as possible. You can always turn down offers later if you feel you don't want same but give yourself the latitude.

Section L. The information is obtained from the student. You should know that summer work will be considered by both CSS and the college in devising the financial aid package. The thinking behind this is that the parent and the student should be contributing toward the educational cost; that it is not solely the responsibility of the parent. Therefore, the CSS will allocate a certain portion of the summer work income towards the college education. The percentages vary depending upon other factors such as the cost of the individual college and the parents' ability to pay.

Notice too that the form includes income accrued even during the school year. No stone is left unturned.

Sections M & N are self-explanatory. The latter section covers divorced or separated parents. If there are special circumstances involved, you will want the college to know about this.

On to page 4 and a break from the numbers. We are up to **Section O.** Here you want to give all information possible relating to the other children or dependents in the household, including what monies have been going toward their education. Review this area carefully. The CSS is interested in seeing what other responsibilities and obligations the parent has, and in what amounts. Don't shortchange yourself.

Section P. Back to the numbers. Self-explanatory. Insert the year of purchase and the purchase price. Obviously, the CSS will then be able to tell how much it appreciated or depreciated in value when they check this figure out against what you supplied earlier. The rest of this section refers to the tax returns.

Section Q relates to the colleges where the analysis is to be sent. What you do here is list the colleges to which you want a copy of the CSS estimation to be forwarded. The CSS code numbers can be found in the back of the booklet you received or from the similar list enclosed with this book. You simply check the appropriate number here. Note that when you are finished, you will be sending the completed FAF form together with the fee as stipulated to the CSS.

Section R is one of the most *important* areas of the FAF. It allows for the enumeration of such special circumstances that will affect eligibility. It used to be that you notified the CSS about this. Now, it goes directly to the colleges to which the student is applying. We'll go into that in a few pages.

Section S covers New York State residents and is self-explanatory. You may have an FAF form without this section or one where there are different assistance programs listed.

Now, this FAF form should be completed and sent to the CSS as close to January 1st as possible. *Don't* send it before January 1st or it will be returned. The key here is to get the form submitted as quickly as possible so that it can be considered well before the deadlines the colleges establish.

Now, it's time to unravel certain things. This is where you get that opportunity. **Section R** becomes the place to do it and you do it directly with the colleges. This is the spot to explain whatever you have to, and don't skimp. You simply get up a letter or piece of paper with the student's name, address and social security number on top and then go into whatever explanations you want. Let me give you a few examples:

One parent was obligated to furnish the child's college education pursuant to his separation agreement. He was now divorced and his wife had remarried. He advised the colleges of the following language in that agreement:

> "Pursuant to the Order of Supreme Court, New York, of ________________(Justice________________presiding/ Index No.________________), Joe Jones (fictitious name), father of Jennifer Jones, is obligated and liable solely for the college education of his daughter, Jennifer Jones, and Jessie Jones is to have no responsibility or liability whatsoever. Joe Jones is required to make all such payments directly to the college. In addition, Joe Jones is obligated for the full child support of Jennifer Jones until completion of college education. Financial conditions and legal obligations under the Court Order may be obtained from ______________________, attorney at_________________."

For the most part, that will aid the father when the college comes a-calling asking to see any records relating to who is supposed to pay for the child's education. Obviously, if the father is making a few bucks but the ex-wife has married a millionaire, the intention is to keep the financial aid people away from the ex-wife who now says she wouldn't contribute anything to the child's college costs.

Other special circumstances can be used, as well.

Suppose, again in a divorce situation, the father has been making huge amounts of child support payments because he just happens to have six kids from three marriages. Here is where you explain that problem. For instance: "Joe Jones has paid a total of $25,352 in child support payments in 1991."

If Mr. Jones has only earned $35,000 from his work, the colleges can quickly see then that Mr. Jones has nothing to give for college. In effect, what you want to do is to explain in detail any unusual expenses, educational and other debts, or special circumstances. Think about this. Don't pass it by too quickly. Most people do. You want to be the exception. You'd be surprised at what you can include with just a little bit of thought. It's a section that is looked at carefully by the colleges. It's your opportunity to explain the financial situation you face so that if help is warranted, it can be made.

I can't stress too strongly the importance of **Section R**. Use it as you would if you had the college's financial aid director sitting in your living room. Be smart, take advantage of it.

After the draft is completed, review all the questions to make sure that everything is answered. Then, transfer the material to the original in pen, make a photocopy for your files, and prepare to mail. Before you do so, you might want to double-check the following:

1) Be sure you have entered the social security number and date of birth.

2) Be sure you have listed at least the colleges to whom you want the analysis sent.

3) Be sure you have checked "Yes" to having the analysis sent to the Department of Education for federal grants and loans.

4) Be sure the Certification section is signed by everyone completing the FAF.

5) Be sure all parts of the FAF are filled in, as requested.

6) Be sure to prepare a check in the amount of the right fee. (Note that the form will be returned if no fee is enclosed)

7) Be sure that the College Scholarship Service address on the front of the mailing envelope, included in the booklet, is completed.

Get this in the mail early, right after January 1st if possible.

Now, what happens next?

After the FAF has been analyzed, the CSS will send you an acknowledgement. It'll take about a month. This acknowledgment will list the colleges to which results have been sent and will provide you with an opportunity to send the forms to additional schools. The section is called the Additional College Request (ACR) Form.

Don't be surprised at what you see and don't have heartburn over the numbers. This is only the College Scholarship Service's analysis and individual colleges will decide what they want to do on their own.

Bear in mind, too, that some schools like to have their own financial aid application completed in addition to the FAF.

As you can readily see, the College Scholarship Service will do its analysis and the college will do theirs. Frankly, this is good for you.

Estimating Costs

Now, much has been made of the so-called Estimate Charts. These are the tables that are found all over the place and which purport to explain the estimated parents' contribution. In short, it tells you what you can expect to receive in financial aid.

I find most of this stuff downright distressing.

First of all, notwithstanding the protestations, an "average family" exists only on charts—not in the real world. I can win most bar bets by saying that your family is not anywhere near the ones used to determine contributions. I think those families with their numbers are drawn from the thin air—very thin air. Therefore, the only way you can know for sure if you're eligible for financial aid is to *apply for it.* Nothing less will do.

For example, I saw one table of figures that gave a general family description as follows: five members of the family consisting of 3 children, 2 parents. The age of the older parent is 45; that's the only parent employed.

With a parental income of $40,000 and assets of $37,000 (I wonder how they saved that much), and student savings of $300 including a summer job worth $700, it was concluded that the parents could contribute some $6,000 toward the child's education for the first year.

Really? Somebody has to be kidding. If the income is $40,000 and therefore, with taxes coming off, it works itself down to $30,000, you mean to say that $6,000 (or one-fifth) goes to the college? What about the basic family needs? Is each member only worth $6,000? From where do they get this number anyway?

So, obviously, most of this means relatively little.

Or, better yet, how about the so-called experts who say that if your income as a parent is $30,000, then you don't qualify for any state aid? Huh? What about if your income is $30,000, you have six children and a dependent handicapped mother? Still don't qualify? Nonsense!

Instead, let me cite some salient, up-to-the-minute facts. Here's a sample financial aid package from Antioch College, Yellow Springs, Ohio. The student budget for one year at Antioch is fixed at $16,450, a nice tidy sum. Now, suppose the adjusted gross family income is some $30,000 and there are assets of some $50,000, with 5 family members and with 2 in college. Antioch will give an aid package of $13,575 toward that $16,450. Not bad.

And remember the prestigious Swarthmore College? Their average aid package last year totaled $12,400.

That's why I say ignore all those tables. Explain your financial situation and whatever difficulties you have to the Director of Financial Aid and include it in **Section R** of the FAF.

As a personal aside, I did that and found that nine times out of ten, I received an understanding and favorable response. The vast majority of financial aid people *want* to help. If a college accepts the student, it will try to make the education affordable.

It is said over and over that you are an individual and that's how your family and financial condition will be viewed by the college financial aid office.

Chapter 4

EVALUATING THE OFFERS

By now, more than half of the Flow Chart should be completed, in one way or another. The filing date of the FAF form is the latest to go in there. As you can see, there are just a few more items to be checked off. One is the school visit. If you did not have an interview at a particular school, then you will most assuredly want to visit that college should it offer a space for your child. Needless to say, this should be done before any final decision is reached.

At this juncture, there is little more that you can do except to wait for the colleges to send in their acceptances, or rejections. This usually arrives around the first week in March although I have seen acceptances repeatedly being offered in January.

Most likely, you will not have a decision on the financial aid package at the time of acceptance. That floats in sometime in April. Thus, you will probably find yourself with acceptances around March 1st, financial aid offers around April 1st, and a final decision required to be made on or before May 1st. You should have sufficient time to evaluate all the information but you can't dilly-dally.

What to do during the few months you are waiting? Make sure that everything has been completed and filed. Contact the various schools, preferably by letter, asking them to advise you whether all items have been received. Based upon the Flow Chart, you should readily see what's missing; go after those at once.

Query. Do you apply any other pressure on the admissions office? Generally not. You don't want to be characterized as a pest. After all, if you have followed what I have outlined in this book, the admissions people should know the student quite well because you will have given them materials not only on time but also in the form they like to see. It can only inure to your benefit.

Needless to say, if you know of any alumnus of a particular college, you can have him/her drop a note to the Director of Admissions extolling the virtues of the applicant. Frankly, I wouldn't get too carried away with this. I have seen where too much pressure leads to adverse decisions. Thus, don't go overboard. Use some restraint. If there is someone who previously attended the school, then there is nothing wrong with having that person use a little bit of influence. However, I am not suggesting out-and-out arm-twisting but rather a gentle push to the effect that the student would be a worthy addition to the college.

Also, you want to be certain that you haven't shortchanged yourself. For example, I expended extra sums of money in order to obtain a favorable financial package. The old axiom is that you only make money with money. Accordingly, whenever I was involved in applying to various schools on behalf of my own children as well as those of others, I did not stint. With one of my kids, I spent some $200 in duplicating a football film to send to college coaches. It helped because the financial offers we received more than paid for the cost of such duplication. Without it, I am sure that we still would have received offers but I believe they would have been of considerably lower value.

The first week in March is when the mailbox begins to fill with letters from colleges. Some say that if you pick up an envelope and it looks as though there is only one sheet of paper inside, it is definitely a rejection but if you have a hefty envelope in your hand, then it's an acceptance because the enrollment materials have been included. I chalk this up to the proverbial "Old Wives Tale." Too often I have seen a thin envelope bearing an acceptance. So, don't be guided by what you hear around you.

Dealing with Acceptance

When you begin receiving acceptances, you should then start the final stage of this entire campaign: finding out everything you can about the individual school so that you will be in the best position possible to make a final decision. A tip: *Don't* wait for the financial aid package; that comes in too close to the May 1st deadline.

Head for the library and look up the books mentioned in Chapter 1. You need to bring with you a Evaluation Chart, which lays out the salient features needed to decide which college has the best attributes for your child's purposes. A copy of this is enclosed. Let's look at what it says:

1) Fill in the material on the college's name, address, phone number and Director of Admissions. Actually, you could have these sheets ready by using the catalogue, admissions application forms, etc., for this information.

2) I like to know when the school was founded. Has it been around for quite some time or is it rather new? I'm not sure what that means but usually the newer schools don't have the facilities and money as yet; of course, some of the older schools may have antiquated equipment. However, I generally like to see a school with a bit of age to it. This makes me feel as though it has not only been around a while but intends to stay in business. A number of colleges have closed recently and competition to get students (except at places like Brown, Harvard and the like) has been keen.

3) Next, I list the affiliation. Again, this is just to distinguish between the public institution and the private. With respect to the latter, I like to know its connections. Some schools are church-related and have heavy endowments because of this. Take Brigham Young University in Utah. The Mormon Church is a fine example of what a powerful backer can do. Its facilities and faculty are both first rate. There's money behind this college and that doesn't hurt.

4) The location of the school. I know this sounds foolish at this point. After all, I should know by now where it is, but it's not so foolish for those who haven't seen the school because the books will indicate whether it is considered in an urban, suburban or rural area, and how many miles from certain downtown or key areas. It helps put the school in better perspective.

5) For the same reason, I like to read what is said about the campus. "Resting on 220 acres of woodland in the heart of the Blue Ridge mountains." This will aid you especially if you haven't visited the school, as yet. In addition, this is the section to list library holdings, an important factor. A college with a low number of library books doesn't say much for its academic environment. I consider this an essential element for a good school.

6) The Faculty section is also a vital one. What you are looking for is the faculty/student ratio. I mentioned this earlier. You would like to know how many students to a teacher. A school that has a 1/25 ratio may not be as good as one that is 1/12. Isn't it better to have one teacher to twelve students rather than one to twenty-five? It's a more individualized, personalized approach. However, don't discount a college simply because of size. I have seen too many instances where larger schools have had a better faculty/student ratio than smaller ones.

Also, you can't ignore the quality of teaching. Check the number of PhDs on campus. It's always helpful to understand the intellectual status of the faculty. Even salaries are discussed in a few books indicating those schools that pay their teachers well. Again, another good barometer. It is said with some satisfaction that the "better teachers will be found at institutions that pay better." There may be some truth in this.

7) Moving along to Enrollment, watch for a few things here. First, you would like to know how many students applied for the freshman class, how many were accepted, and how many actually enrolled.

The figures, you see, will be last year's, or even a few years ago. No matter. It gives you some indication as to what the school receives in applications against the number it decides to accept against how many enroll. A school like Duke will see a large number of applicants but only a small number of acceptances doled out. Its enrollment rate, obviously, is quite high and they have no problems in filling vacancies for the incoming class.

Enrollment also says something about the students as well. Some books list the male/female ratio, some the number of students from a given area as opposed to those from outside, and the total enrollment in the school.

8) The 1991 Freshman Class is simply an example. You're looking at whatever freshman class is listed in the books and what you're primarily trying to find here is the number of returning freshmen. These books report how many freshmen come back for their sophomore year including how many students who began with the college eventually graduate. The higher the numbers, the better. You're seeking stability. A school that indicates only 45% of the freshman class returning for the second year and only 35% continuing to graduation, says a lot about the school; perhaps more about the students it accepts. There's something wrong and although you may not be able to find out exactly what (it's usually a combination of things), you will have at least seen a warning sign).

By now, someone out there is saying, "All this stuff is interesting but why didn't I do this the first time I went to the library?" Good question, and the answer is that you didn't have time and you didn't want to waste hours in analyzing *all* the schools before you made application and received acceptances. Besides, in the intervening months you no doubt have learned a lot about the colleges you eventually applied to by filling out the forms, staying in contact with the schools and even visiting them. It's easier to complete the picture now than it would have been last October.

9) We come to the students. Here you will see a myriad of information: where the students come from, what majors they take, where the preponderance of people go afterwards, etc. There may also be material about job placement and the number of foreign students, minorities and the like, not to mention a listing of intercollegiate sports, extra-curricular activities, fraternities, sororities and clubs.

10)Costs vary and much of what you see here can be discounted. The numbers reflect those costs at the time the book was written. Your best bet is to refer to the *current* catalogues which will provide you with the actual figures.

11)These books break down how many freshmen receive financial aid and in what form (grants, loan, work study), and how many students overall receive financial aid. It's a rather interesting indicator of what you may or may not see from the financial aid office.

12) Finally, most books will rate the schools. They range from "Highly Competitive" to "Very Competitive" to "Competitive" to "Less Competitive." Some books will use letter sequences or other markings to distinguish a University of California at Berkeley, which is "Highly Competitive," to a Temple University which is "Less Competitive."

Once this form is completed, I then like to read some of the other books (for example, Fiske and Birnbach) to get some gossip, perhaps more of a flavor about the school itself. Needless to say, the student should be reading this, as well. As I mentioned earlier, these books tend to dwell on the quality of life at the college, with a few tidbits of extraneous information (such as the nearest pizza place) thrown in to help fill out the picture of the particular school.

As the acceptances begin rolling in (and I hope that it will come this way), you can start evaluating the colleges, one against the other, based on the information you now have. I realize that the picture will not be complete without the financial aid package, but you must do the best you can under the circumstances. However, don't rule out any college until the financial aid offer arrives.

If, of course, you haven't received any response from the college admissions office by the middle of March, then contact the Director of Admissions to find out what's happening. Don't wait. Do it immediately. You won't have enough time remaining to evaluate properly your options before the May 1st deadline. Perhaps a letter went astray or something is fouled up in Central Filing. Don't take chances. Stay on top of the matter. You've come too far to let down now.

Dealing with Rejection

What happens if you do get a rejection? If you have followed what I have been preaching in this book, I will bet that you won't see many rejections, if at all. At least, I hope you won't. There is not much you can do with a turn-down except to drop it in the circular file. Most rejections don't warrant an appeal. For example, a school like Brown last year received some 11,717 applicants for only 1,411 places in the freshman class. Therefore, your child is in the same position as 10,000 others. A "No" from that college is final.

But, another school having fewer applicants might reject the student with a proviso that he be added to the waiting list. It cuts a number of different ways.

Penn State has a main campus at University Park, Pennsylvania, with a number of satellite campuses around the state. Your child might not be accepted at the main campus but might be at one of the satellite campuses. It's still an acceptance...of sorts.

By the same token, an acceptance could be at one of the campuses other than the main one for the freshman year only, with transfer to the University Park campus the sophomore year. So, it is not a rejection in the purest sense.

Consider Bloomsburg University, also in Pennsylvania. They have classes all year long. The student might not be accepted to the fall term commencing in September but could be accepted to a term starting that summer or, in fact, to the one next February. You have to review all rejections against the school's applied for/spaces available ratio.

If it's a clear-cut rejection with no waiting list or other alternatives or conditions, as I have outlined above, I suggest that you face the reality of the situation and concentrate on the other schools. Too many parents agonize over a rejection as if it were life and death, and they begin contacting everyone from the President of the Alumni Association to the Governor of the State. It won't really do you any good. At most colleges, the admissions office is rather autonomous with its own way of doing things. You're simply wasting your time and energy when they could be put to better use by working to get your child into a school where there's a stronger chance of acceptance.

I've seen parents turn cartwheels over the child's not getting into Harvard, when the student has only an average G.P.A. and SAT score.

"Yes, I know that and I know there are a lot of applicants, but, after all, he was President of his class and he was voted the one most likely to succeed."

That's very good indeed but his high school wasn't exactly on Harvard's level either and the college is not handing out acceptances based on someone being a class president, no matter what the yearbook says. This is not like applying to a fraternity or camera club. Competition for the better schools is fierce and you have to recognize this fact.

The "Hidden" Question

There is one question that never seems to be asked, yet in today's troubled times, it may be one of the most important of all. How safe is the campus? This is especially true for females.

Every day the newspapers pick up an account of a rape or other crime committed on a college campus. Some are more violent than others. One need only remember the serial killer who floated around that college in Florida last year or the rapist who attacked coeds at the large upstate New York university recently. And, there are many more that are never reported.

By the same token, there is the flip side where Penn State, ensconced in the hills of central Pennsylvania, had the reputation for being the safest campus in the country, a reason why State College had been dubbed Happy Valley.

The question of campus security is a vital one and one which should not be ignored. It is true that it is much more difficult in large urban areas where in many instances, fine universities are surrounded by decayed, poverty-stricken areas. But, just because the college is in a urban center doesn't mean it is totally unsafe and conversely, a school in an idyllic rural setting is not necessarily free of crime.

What can you do about it? You can ask questions. It belongs on the list. The best person to ask is the student herself. When visiting a college campus, ask students about the safety of their environment. Find out what has been the major problems in recent years.

Secondly, check the school newspaper. Most of them are student-written and student-run, and they have a tendency to report everything, no matter how controversial or damaging to the university. The college administrators may not like what is being printed but you will get straight answers. Stop by the newspaper office and talk to the people there.

You can also check the local police station for crime reports and their opinions, although generally you may receive a more rosier picture than is readily apparent. The same applies to the university people. They will not exactly reveal everything. After all, they are looking for you to attend the school. They are not looking for reasons to dissuade you.

When walking around the campus, keep your eyes open for security guards, both on foot and in vehicles. This will give you an idea of how the campus is being patrolled, or if not at all.

Check the bulletin boards, both in dormitories and on campus posts. See what, if any, lectures are being given on what subjects. It may give you a clue as to the seriousness of the university in combating campus crime.

Your child may want to visit the school again, perhaps to meet with some of the teachers, to attend a class. Most schools will arrange all this and you need only contact the admissions office for additional information. They will be happy to accommodate you. Remember, they operate on a two-pronged system: First, they try to interest a student in their school and to extract an application. That's step number one. Then, if they accept the student, they must get that student to enroll. Keep in mind that they are out there with plenty of other colleges vying for applicants. So, they will be most cooperative.

Evaluating the offers is a highly personal matter. No one else can do it for you. Your child has to talk with current students, past students and those who are thinking of joining him as a freshman. Actually, I wouldn't lose too much sleep over the situation. It's a lot of fun. Keep in mind, though, that you are evaluating offers for those colleges that *want* your child. What a nice position to be in.

Chapter 5

CUSTOMARY FIRST YEAR PROBLEMS & EXPENSES

This is a wide open area. Therefore, I cannot possibly cover all the problems the student might have in the initial year. I can only give you an idea of what sorts of difficulties he might encounter.

For many students, there is an enormous gap between high school with its structured way of life and college which is generally unstructured. For example, the high school student reports at a certain time in the morning and stays there until a certain time in the afternoon. There will be different subjects in different classrooms with different teachers but by and large, it is a regimented existence. The student goes to school five days a week with a one week break between semesters.

College life, though, is not that. Whether the student is living at home or commuting to campus, the life style is basically unstructured and unregimented. The student might go to school only a few hours a day, and it's not necessarily every day. Schedules are prepared based upon courses for which the student has registered and as a result, you might find that your child is home more than he is in class. Breaks between terms are usually a month.

All this free time is supposed to enable the student to do some real studying instead of the couple of hours after dinner each night when he was in high school. Can you imagine what a full day off can do for you in your own work?

The problem is that the adjustment from the prison-like atmosphere of high school to the independence of college can take its toll.

There are students who just can't handle all this unsupervised time and wind up doing too many things except studying. The purpose of college is to get an education and that doesn't mean solely a social education or one in how to sleep successfully. Thus, the problems you may see in the first year will be varied.

According to the Dean of Students at various colleges, this mainly has to do with budgeting time. After some twelve years of structured classrooms (kindergarten through high school), the student now has an environment where he must be able to set priorities. Many have trouble the first year in doing this. There is just so much freedom that some students find themselves unable to cope with it. They take jobs or join social groups or begin hobbies or just sit around with fellow students and "shoot the breeze."

Budgeting of time and setting of priorities are the most crucial elements. The student can find help by seeking out the office of the Dean of Students or his advisor; they would be happy to aid. Remember, you are dealing with an adjustment to the beginning of adult life with all its responsibilities and obligations.

The next area relates to money. Most parents and students do not realize what kind of expenses can crop up. These vary greatly among schools. There are direct educational costs like tuition, fees, books and supplies, and then there are living costs like room, board, transportation and personal expenses. You must also consider whether the student plans on living at home and commuting to the college or residing on or near the campus. If you have any unusual expenses such as child care or ongoing medical needs, you must figure this into your budget, as well.

That's the key. You have to lay out on paper what the year will cost. If the student plans to live on campus, you should estimate the cost of the round trips he will make from the school to the home. Colleges usually say there will be three round trips during the year. Students living at home should figure the cost of daily transportation to the college.

As far as books are concerned, the average figure for the freshman year is approximately $400. Used books are available and the student should try and buy those.

There is a telephone to consider as well as laundry, haircuts, clothing, personal items, etc., not to mention what students living away take to the campus. In that respect, here is a list of first year items that the average student may require:

Freshman Items

- Alarm Clock
- All-Weather Boots
- Bathing Suit
- Bedspread & Curtains
- Blankets
- Book Bag
- Bucket for Toilet Articles
- Casual Attire for Class
- Clothes for all Seasons
- Coins for Laundry
- Desk Lamp
- Drying Rack
- Eating Utensils
- Extension Cord
- Hand Tools (hammer, pliers)
- Hot Plate
- Iron
- Laundry Bag
- Mattress Pad
- Needed Medicines
- Paper Plates & Cups
- Pillow
- Posters
- Plants
- School Supplies
- Radio
- Rain Jacket
- Sewing Kit
- Sheets
- Snacks
- Sporting Gear
- Stereo
- Toilet Articles
- Towels
- Washcloths & Handtowels

And this all costs money!

Budget Plans

Incidentally, there are ways that college costs can be budgeted through various groups. Many of them provide a monthly prepayment plan designed to relieve the pressure of "lump sum" payments by allowing parents to spread annual educational costs over a period of months without borrowing money or paying interest charges. Most charge a single annual application fee of something like $30 or $40 regardless of the amount of the budget. There are no additional interest or finance charges. The cost usually includes a life benefit coverage for the parent at no charge.

Most of the information can be obtained from the individual college's business office, and there are two organizations you might want to check:

Academic Management Services
111 Central Avenue
Pawtucket, RI 02861
(800) 556-6684

EFI-Fund Management
2700 Saunders Road
Prospect Heights, IL 60070
(800) 323-8399

There are other groups that provide a private loan arrangement or prepayment monthly budget plan which covers money to meet educational expenses as they fall due. This enables families to budget the costs through monthly installments. Some have closed-end loans available for 1, 2, 3 or 4 year programs with loan repayment options extended up to 8 years for the 4- year program. Two companies you might want to look at are:

The Tuition Plan
57 Regional Drive
Concord, NH 03301
(603) 228-1161

New Insured Tuition Plan
53 Beacon Street
Boston, MA 02108
(617) 742-3911

Most of the programs are available to students or parents regardless of demonstrated need, and range from monthly prepayment plans to extended loan plans.

Keep in mind that payment of financial aid is made at the time a student actually enrolls. The financial aid office can tell you how the payments from each aid source will be made to you. Obviously, if you have questions at any stage of the process, ask until you get an answer. Asking questions won't make you seem stupid; not asking a question that is important could cost you money.

A Final Note

College experience is not only the student's experience but the entire family's.

Understanding the intense interest you have in the welfare of your child from the beginning, you are looking for a superb faculty, a caring administration and a dedicated staff.

Go to Parents Weekends. Become a member of the Parents Association. It will afford you the opportunity to become even more involved in college life by providing a better means of communication among parents, the administration and the student body.

SAMPLE FORMS

PROFILE

A. Co-Ed____ Ratio______

B. Location:

Commute _______

Campus _________ How Far?_________ Weather ___________________

C. Environment:

Small _______

Medium _______

Large _______

Rural _______

Suburban _______

Urban _______

D. Religious Affiliation:____

E. Course of Study:____

F. Extra Curricular/Facilities/Social:____

____

____

____

G. Grade Point Average: ________

H. Standardized Scores: PSAT _________ SAT __________ ACT ________

APPLICATION FLOW CHART

College	Information Received	Application Deadline	Application Filed	Transcript	Teacher Recommendations	SAT Filed	FAF Filed	Visit	School Decision	Financial Package	Final Decision	Deposit

Agnes Scott • Alfred • Allegheny • American University • Antioch • Bard • Bates • Beloit • Bennington • Boston University • Brandeis • Bryn Mawr • Bucknell • Carleton • Case Western Reserve • Centenary College • Centre • Claremont McKenna • Clark University • Coe • Colby-Sawyer • Colgate • Colorado College • Connecticut College • Cornell College • Denison • University of Denver • DePauw • Dickinson • Drew • Duke • Earlham • Eckerd • Elmira • Emory • Fairfield • Fisk • Fordham • Franklin & Marshall • Gettysburg • Goucher • Grinnell • Guilford • Hamilton • Hampden-Sydney • Hampshire • Hartwick • Haverford • Hobart • Hood • Kalamazoo • Kenyon • Knox • Lafayette • Lawrence • Lehigh • Lewis and Clark • Linfield • Macalester • Manhattan • Manhattanville • Mills • Millsaps • Morehouse • Mount Holyoke • Muhlenberg • New York University • Oberlin • Occidental • Ohio Wesleyan • Pitzer • Pomona • University of Puget Sound • Randolph-Macon • Randolph Macon Woman's • University of Redlands • Reed College • Rensselaer Polytechnic • Rhodes • Rice • University of Richmond • Ripon • University of Rochester • Rollins • St. Lawrence • St. Olaf • Salem • Sarah Lawrence • Scripps • Simmons • Skidmore • Smith • University of the South • University of Southern California • Southern Methodist • Southwestern • Spelman • Stetson • Susquehanna • Swarthmore • Texas Christian • Trinity College • Trinity University • Tulane • Tulsa • Union • Ursinus • Valparaiso • Vanderbilt • Vassar • Wake Forest • Washington College • George Washington • Washington and Lee • Wells • Wesleyan • Western Maryland • Wheaton • Whitman • Willamette • William Smith • Williams • Wooster • Worcester Polytechnic

APPLICATION FOR UNDERGRADUATE ADMISSION

The colleges and universities listed above encourage the use of this application. Please type or print in ink.

PERSONAL DATA

Legal name: STUDENT (*Last*) Stuart (*First*) S. (*Middle (complete)*) ______ (*Jr., etc.*) Male (*Sex*)

Prefer to be called: ____________ (nickname) Former last name(s) if any: ____________

Are you applying as a freshman ☒ or transfer student ☐ ? For the term beginning: September 1992

Permanent home address: 100 Main Street (*Number and Street*)

Anytown (*City or Town*) ______ (*County*) U.S.A. (*State*) 00000 (*Zip*) State of legal residence ____________

If different from the above, please give your mailing address for all admission correspondence:

Mailing address: ____________ (*Number and Street*)

____________ (*City or Town*) ____________ (*State*) ____________ (*Zip*)

Telephone at mailing address: ______ (*Area Code*) / ______ (*Number*) Permanent home telephone: ______ (*Area Code*) / ______ (*Number*)

Birthdate: ______ (*Month Day Year*) Citizenship: U.S. ☐ Permanent Resident U.S. ☐ Other ☐ ______ (*Country*) Visa type ______

Possible area(s) of academic concentration/major: Pre-Medicine ______ or undecided ☐

Special college or division if applicable: ____________

Possible career or professional plans: Medicine or undecided ☐

Will you be a candidate for financial aid? Yes X No ______ If yes, the appropriate form(s) ~~was~~/will be filed on: January 1982

The following items are optional:

Social Security number, if any: ☐☐☐ ☐☐ ☐☐☐☐

Place of birth: ______ (*City*) ______ (*State*) ______ (*Country*) Marital status: ______ Height: ______ Weight: ______

Parents' country of birth: Mother ______ Father ______

What is your first language, if other than English? ______

How would you describe yourself: (Please check one)

- ☐ American Indian or Alaskan Native
- ☐ Asian or Pacific Islander (including Indian subcontinent)
- ☐ Black (non-Hispanic)
- ☐ Hispanic (including Puerto Rican)
- ☐ White, Anglo, Caucasian (non-Hispanic)
- ☐ Other (Specify)

EDUCATIONAL DATA

School you attend now Anytown High School ACT/CEEB code number 1234567

Address ______ (*City*) ______ (*State*) ______ (*Zip Code*)

Date of secondary school graduation June 1992 Is your school public? X private? ______ parochial? ______

College advisor: ______ (*Name*) ______ (*Position*) School telephone: ______ (*Area Code*) / ______ (*Number*)

APP

List all other secondary schools, including summer schools and programs you have attended beginning with ninth grade.

Name of School	Location (City, State, Zip)	Dates Attended

List all colleges at which you have taken courses for credit and list names of courses on a separate sheet. Please have a transcript sent from each institution as soon as possible.

Name of College	Location (City, State, Zip)	Degree Candidate?	Dates Attended

If not currently attending school, please check here: ☐ Describe in detail, on a separate sheet, your activities since last enrolled.

TEST INFORMATION. Be sure to note the tests required for each institution to which you are applying. The official scores from the appropriate testing agency must be submitted to each institution as soon as possible. Please list your test plans below.

	Scholastic Aptitude Test (SAT)	Achievement Tests (ACH)		Subject		American College Test (ACT)
Dates taken or	11/91: 990	Physics: 530				
to be taken		Mathematics,	English	(Jan.	1993)	

FAMILY

Mother's full name: ____________ Is she living? ____________

Home address if different from yours: ____________

Occupation: ____________ (Describe briefly) ____________ (Name of business or organization)

Name of college (if any): ____________ Degree: ____________ Year: ____________

Name of professional or graduate school (if any): ____________ Degree: ____________ Year: ____________

Father's full name: ____________ Is he living? ____________

Home address if different from yours: ____________

Occupation: ____________ (Describe briefly) ____________ (Name of business or organization)

Name of college (if any): ____________ Degree: ____________ Year: ____________

Name of professional or graduate school (if any): ____________ Degree: ____________ Year: ____________

If not with both parents, with whom do you make your permanent home: ____________

Please check if parents are separated ☐ divorced ☐

Please give names and ages of your brothers or sisters. If they have attended college, give the names of the institutions attended, degrees, and approximate dates:

____

____

ACADEMIC HONORS

Briefly describe any scholastic distinctions or honors you have won beginning with ninth grade:

Bill Long Award as Outstanding Student. 3.2 Grade Point Average with 3 accelerated courses in Mathematics and Biology

EXTRACURRICULAR AND PERSONAL ACTIVITIES

Please list your principal extracurricular, community, and family activities and hobbies in the order of their interest to you. Include specific events and/or major accomplishments such as musical instrument played, varsity letters earned, etc. Please (√) in the right column those activities you hope to pursue in college.

Activity	Grade level or post-secondary (p.s.)					Approximate time spent		Positions held, honors won, or letters earned	Do you plan to participate in college?
	9	10	11	12	P.S.	Hours per week	Weeks per year		
Football	X	x	x	x					

WORK EXPERIENCE

List any job (including summer employment) you have held during the past three years.

Specific nature of work	Employer	Approximate dates of employment	Approximate no. of hours spent per week
Clamming	Self	Summer	30

In the space provided below, briefly discuss which of these activities (extracurricular and personal activities or work experience) has had the most meaning for you, and why.

PERSONAL STATEMENT

This personal statement helps us become acquainted with you in ways different from courses, grades, test scores and other objective data. *It enables you to demonstrate your ability to organize thoughts and express yourself. Please write an essay about one of the topics listed below.* You may attach extra pages (same size, please) if your essay exceeds the limits of this page.

1) Evaluate a significant experience or achievement that has special meaning to you.
2) Discuss some issue of personal, local, or national concern and its importance to you.
3) Indicate a person who has had a significant influence on you, and describe that influence.

Building my own clamboat
(see attached)

I understand that: (1) it is my responsibility to report any changes in my schedule to the colleges to which I am applying, and (2) if I am an Early Decision Candidate, that I must attach a letter with this application notifying that college of my intent.

My signature below indicates that all information contained in my application is complete, factually correct, and honestly presented.

Signature ______________________ Date ______________________

These colleges are committed to administer all educational policies and activities without discrimination on the basis of race, color, religion, national or ethnic origin, age, handicap, or sex. The admissions process at private undergraduate institutions is exempt from the federal regulation implementing Title IX of the Education Amendments of 1972.

CSS Code List

ALABAMA

1003 Alabama A & M University
1006 Alabama State University
Auburn University:
1005 —Auburn
1036 —Montgomery
3231 Bessemer State Tech. College
1064 Birmingham-Southern College
3331 C. A. Fredd State Tech. College
1262 Gadsden State Community Coll.
1303 Huntingdon College
1736 Jacksonville State University
1352 Jefferson State Comm. College
1737 Livingston University
1468 Miles College
1515 Mobile College
1586 Oakwood College
1302 Samford University
1723 Southeastern Bible College
1733 Spring Hill College
1739 Stillman College
1800 Talladega College
1738 Troy State University, Troy
1813 Tuskegee University
The University of Alabama:
1856 —Birmingham
1032 —School of Dentistry
1992 —School of Medicine
1990 —School of Optometry
1854 —Huntsville
1830 —Tuscaloosa
1004 University of Montevallo
1735 University of North Alabama
1880 University of South Alabama

ALASKA

0276 **Alaska Commission on Postsecondary Education**
4201 Alaska Pacific University
4224 Association Village Council Presidents
4373 Kenai Peninsula College
4509 Matanuska-Susitna Comm. Coll.
4498 St. Herman's Theological Seminary
4742 Sheldon Jackson College
8797 Tlingit and Haida Central Council
University of Alaska:
4896 —Anchorage
4866 —Fairbanks
4897 —Southeast

ARIZONA

4007 Arizona State University
4013 Arizona Western College
4122 Central Arizona College
7347 Chandler-Gilbert Comm. Coll. Ctr.
4097 Cochise College
DeVry Institute of Technology:
4277 —Continuing Students
0370 —New/Transfer Students
4297 Eastern Arizona College
4305 Embry-Riddle Aero. Univ.
4338 Glendale Community College
4331 Grand Canyon University
4513 Mesa Community College
4495 Mohave Community College
4550 Navajo Community College
4006 Northern Arizona University
4606 Phoenix College
7719 Phoenix Institute of Technology
4623 Pima Community College
4631 Prescott College
4904 Rio Salado Community College
4755 Scottsdale Community College
4734 South Mountain Comm. College
7903 Universal Technical Institute
4832 University of Arizona
4996 Yavapai College:
4721 —Verde Campus

ARKANSAS

6009 Arkansas College
6011 Arkansas State University
6267 Harding University
6321 John Brown University
University of Arkansas:
6866 —Fayetteville
6004 —Pine Bluff
6012 University of Central Arkansas

CALIFORNIA

4213 Academy of Art College
4002 Allan Hancock College
7024 American Academy of Dramatic Arts, West
4715 American Coll. for the Applied Arts
7005 American Conservatory Theatre
4216 American Film Institute—Center for Advanced Film Studies
4004 American River College
4005 Antelope Valley College
Antioch University:
7032 —Marina Del Rey
7586 —Santa Barbara
4009 Art Center College of Design
7164 Art Inst. of Southern California
4596 Azusa Pacific University
4015 Bakersfield College
4020 Barstow College
4021 Bethany College
4017 Biola University
4236 Brooks College
4228 Brooks Inst. of Photo. Art & Science
4239 Bryan Coll. of Court Reporting
4226 Butte College
4084 Cabrillo College
4094 California Baptist College
4031 California Coll. of Arts & Crafts
4032 California Coll. of Podiatric Med.
7230 California Culinary Academy
5221 California Family Study Center
4049 California Institute of the Arts
4807 California Inst. of Integral Studies
4034 California Inst. of Technology
4088 California Lutheran University
4035 California Maritime Academy
California Sch. of Professional Psych.:
4129 —Alhambra
4128 —Berkeley-Alameda
4148 —Fresno
4142 —San Diego
California State Universities:
4110 —Bakersfield
4048 —Chico
4098 —Dominguez Hills
4312 —Fresno
4589 —Fullerton
4011 —Hayward
4345 —Humboldt
4389 —Long Beach
4399 —Los Angeles (CSUC)
4707 —Northridge
4082 —Pomona (Polytechnic)
4671 —Sacramento
4099 —San Bernardino
4682 —San Diego
4684 —San Francisco
4687 —San Jose
4038 —San Luis Obispo (Polytechnic)
4924 —San Marcos
4723 —Sonoma
4713 —Stanislaus
4802 California Western School of Law
4109 Canada College
4083 Cerritos College
4027 Cerro Coso Comm. College
4725 Chabot College
4046 Chaffey Community College
4047 Chapman College
8301 Charles R. Drew Univ. of Med. & Sci.
4069 Christ College, Irvine
4150 Christian Heritage College
4051 Citrus College
4052 City College of San Francisco
4053 Claremont Graduate School
4054 Claremont McKenna College
7182 Cleveland Chiropractic College
4086 Coastline Community College
4057 Cogswell Polytechnical College
4132 Coleman College
4118 College of Alameda
4117 College of the Canyons
4085 College of the Desert
College of Marin:
4361 —Indian Valley Campus
4061 —Marin Campus
4063 College of Notre Dame
8550 Coll. of Osteopathic Med. of the Pacific
4100 College of the Redwoods
4070 College of San Mateo
4071 College of the Sequoias
4087 College of the Siskiyous
4108 Columbia College
7213 Columbia College—Hollywood
4078 Compton Community College
4804 Condie Coll. of Bus. & Tech.
4943 Contra Costa College
4121 Cosumnes River College
4126 Crafton Hills College
4101 Cuesta College
4252 Cuyamaca College
4104 Cypress College
8279 Daniel Freeman Hosp. Paramedic Sch.
4286 De Anza College
DeVry Institute of Technology:
4799 —Continuing Students
0366 —New/Transfer Students
4295 Diablo Valley College
4284 Dominican Coll. of San Rafael
4296 East Los Angeles College
4302 El Camino College
4275 Empire College
4273 Evergreen Valley College
Fashion Inst. of Design & Merchandising:
8663 —Costa Mesa
4457 —Los Angeles
4066 —San Diego
4461 —San Francisco
4460 —Sherman Oaks
4318 Feather River Comm. Coll. Dist.
4316 Fielding Institute
4315 Foothill College
4311 Fresno City College
4616 Fresno Pacific College
4313 Fuller Theological Seminary
4314 Fullerton College
4678 Gavilan College
4327 Glendale Community College
4329 Golden Gate University
4436 Golden State Business College
4339 Golden West College
4334 Grossmont College
4340 Hartnell College
4341 Harvey Mudd College
Heald Colleges/Institutes:
4145 —Fresno (4C's College)
4452 —Hayward (Business)
0468 —Hayward (Technology)
4470 —Martinez (Technology)
4451 —Oakland (Business)
4453 —Rancho Cordova (Business)
4270 —Rancho Cordova (Technology)
4637 —Rohnert Park (Business)
4458 —San Francisco (Business)
4343 —San Francisco (Technology)
4459 —San Jose (Business)
7434 —San Jose (Technology)
4140 —Stockton (Business)
4462 —Walnut Creek (Business)
4445 Hollywood Scriptwriting Institute
4059 Holy Names College
4346 Humphreys College
4358 Imperial Valley College
ITT Technical Institute:
4629 —Buena Park
4975 —Carson
9638 —La Mesa
3835 —Sacramento
8224 —San Bernardino
4643 —Van Nuys
9475 —West Covina
4357 Jewish Vocational Service
4365 John F. Kennedy University
4371 Kelsey-Jenny College
4655 King's River Comm. College
3695 La Jolla Academy
4380 La Sierra University
4420 Lake Tahoe Community Coll.
4406 Laney College
4383 Lassen College
4527 Life Bible College
3401 Life Chiropractic College West
4062 Loma Linda University
4388 Long Beach City College
4391 Los Angeles City College
4393 Los Angeles Coll. of Chiropractic
4405 Los Angeles County Medical Center School of Nursing
4395 Los Angeles Harbor College
4404 Los Angeles Mission College
4398 Los Angeles Pierce College
4409 Los Angeles Southwest College
4400 Los Angeles Trade-Tech. Coll.
4401 Los Angeles Valley College
4396 Los Medanos College
4403 Loyola Marymount University
4397 Loyola University Sch. of Law
4515 Marymount College
4517 Mendocino College
4483 Menlo College
4500 Merced College
4523 Merit College, Van Nuys
4502 Merritt College, Oakland
4485 Mills College
4582 Mira Costa College
7587 Mission College, Santa Clara
4486 Modesto Junior College
4507 Monterey Inst. of Int'l Studies
4490 Monterey Peninsula College
4512 Moorpark College
Mount Saint Mary's College:
4493 —Chalon Campus
4520 —Doheny Campus
4494 Mount San Antonio College
4501 Mount San Jacinto College
4468 Musicians' Institute
4530 Napa Valley College
National Education Center:
7783 —Sawyer Campus
4753 —Skadron College of Business
9013 National Hispanic University
4557 National University
4555 New College of California:
7655 —Law
4540 Northrop University
4581 Occidental College
4579 Ohlone College
4584 Orange Coast College
4394 Otis/Parsons Art Institute
4591 Oxnard College
4614 Pacific Christian College
4638 Pacific Grad. Sch. Psych.
4612 Pacific Oaks College
4600 Pacific Union College
4561 Palmer College Chiropractic, West
4603 Palo Verde College
4602 Palomar College
4604 Pasadena City College
4620 Patten College
Pepperdine University:
4326 —Los Angeles Campus
4630 —Malibu Campus
8159 —School of Law
Phillips Junior College:
4962 —Condie Campus
4548 —Northridge Campus
4619 Pitzer College
4605 Point Loma Nazarene College
4607 Pomona College
4608 Porterville College
4689 Rancho Santiago College
4663 Rio Hondo Comm. College
4658 Riverside Comm. College
4670 Sacramento City College
4747 Saddleback College
4675 Saint Mary's Coll. of California
4750 Samuel Merritt College of Nursing
4679 San Bernardino Valley College
4681 San Diego City College
7547 San Diego Community College, Continuing Education Centers
4735 San Diego Mesa College
4728 San Diego Miramar College
4873 San Fernando Valley Coll. of Law
4036 San Francisco Art Institute
4722 San Francisco Comm. Coll. Centers
4744 San Francisco Conserv. of Music
4706 San Joaquin Delta College
4756 San Jose Christian College
4686 San Jose City College
4690 Santa Barbara City College
4851 Santa Clara University
4691 Santa Monica College
4692 Santa Rosa Junior College
4347 Saybrook Institute
4693 Scripps College
4696 Shasta College
4697 Sierra Community College
4698 Simpson College, Redding
4746 Skyline College
4930 Solano Community College
4701 Southern California Coll., Costa Mesa
7904 Southern California College of Chiropractic
4392 Southern California College of Optometry, Fullerton
7829 Southern California Inst. of Architecture
4726 Southwestern College
4703 Southwestern Univ. Sch. of Law
4704 Stanford University:
7832 —School of Law
4758 —School of Medicine
4820 Taft College
4411 The Master's College
4828 Thomas Aquinas College
4039 United States Internat'l Univ.
University of California:
4833 —Berkeley, Undergraduate
4908 —Berkeley, Graduate, Law, Optometry
4834 —Davis
4139 —Grad. Sch. of Management
4902 —School of Law
4886 —School of Medicine
4818 Veterinary Medicine
4859 —Irvine
4884 —School of Medicine
4837 —Los Angeles (UCLA)
4890 School of Dentistry
8818 School of Management
4879 —School of Medicine
9605 —Univ. Extension
4839 —Riverside
4836 —San Diego
4883 —Medicine
4840 —San Francisco, Allied Health Professions
7908 —Dentistry
4885 —Medicine
7892 —Nursing
7893 —Pharmacy
7894 —Physical Therapy
4342 —San Francisco, Hastings College of Law
4835 —Santa Barbara
4860 —Santa Cruz
4876 University of Judaism
4381 University of La Verne
4065 University of the Pacific:
7895 —McGeorge School of Law
4892 —School of Dentistry
4449 —School of Physical Therapy
4848 University of Redlands:
4251 —Whitehead Center
4849 University of San Diego:
4891 —School of Law
4850 University of San Francisco:
7902 —Law
4852 Univ. of Southern California:
7898 —Dental Hygiene, Junior
4893 —School of Dentistry
4492 —School of Law
4882 —School of Medicine
7900 —School of Pharmacy
4708 —School of Physical Therapy
4918 —Other Grad. Studies
4872 University of West LA School of Law
4931 Ventura College
4932 Victor Valley College
7711 Vista College
3313 Watterson College, Oxnard Campus
4970 West Coast Christian College
4966 West Coast University
4056 West Hills Community College
4964 West Los Angeles College
4958 West Valley College
Western State University College of Law:
4969 —Fullerton
4973 —San Diego
4950 Westmont College
4952 Whittier College:
4028 —School of Law
4955 Woodbury University
4981 World College West
4965 Wright Institute, Berkeley
4994 Yuba College

COLORADO

4001 Adams State College
4659 Colorado Christian University
4072 Colorado College
7150 Colorado Institute of Art
4073 Colorado School of Mines
4075 Colorado State University
4310 Fort Lewis College
4505 Metropolitan State Coll. of Denver
4656 Regis University
University of Colorado:
4841 —Boulder
4874 —Colorado Springs
4875 —Denver
4842 University of Denver
4074 University of Northern Colorado
4611 University of Southern Colorado
4946 Western State Coll. of Colorado

CONNECTICUT

3001 Albertus Magnus College
3656 Asnuntuck Community College
3121 Briarwood College
3093 Bridgeport Engineering Institute
3104 Bridgeport Hospital Sch. of Nrsg.
3898 Central Connecticut State Univ.
3284 Connecticut College
3966 Eastern Connecticut State Univ.
3390 Fairfield University
3421 Greater Hartford Comm. College
3425 Greater New Haven St. Tech Coll.
3431 Hartford College for Women
3768 Hartford State Technical College
3446 Housatonic Community College
3544 Manchester Community College
3550 Mattatuck Community College
3551 Middlesex Community College
3528 Mitchell College
3558 Mohegan Community College
3652 Northwestern Conn. Comm. Coll.
3678 Norwalk Community College
3675 Norwalk State Tech. College
3556 Ona M. Wilcox Sch. of Nursing
3699 Paier College of Art
3716 Quinebaug Valley Comm. Coll.
3712 Quinnipiac College
3780 Sacred Heart University
3781 Saint Francis Hosp. Sch. of Nrsg.
3754 Saint Joseph College
3798 Saint Mary's Hosp. Sch. of Nrsg.
3789 Saint Vincent's Med. Ctr. Sch. of Nrsg.
3792 South Central Community Coll.
3662 Southern Connecticut St. Univ.
9905 Technical Careers Institute
3698 Teikyo Post University
3654 Thames Valley State Tech. Coll.
3899 Trinity College
3897 Tunxis Community College
3914 University of Bridgeport
3915 University of Connecticut:
7867 —School of Law
7868 —School of Social Work
3436 University of Hartford
3663 University of New Haven
3978 Waterbury State Technical Coll.
3959 Wesleyan University
3350 Western Connecticut State Univ.
Yale University:
3213 —Continuing Undergraduates only
3987 —New Freshmen & Transfers only
3940 —School of Nursing

DELAWARE

0583 **Delaware State Scholarship Program**
5153 Delaware State College
Delaware Technical & Community Coll.:
5204 —Stanton
5201 —Terry
5154 —Wilmington
5255 Goldey-Beacom College
5811 University of Delaware
5894 Wesley College
5081 Widener University

DISTRICT OF COLUMBIA

5007 American University:
5007 —Washington College of Law
5104 Catholic University of America
5705 Corcoran School of Art
5240 Gallaudet University
5246 George Washington University:
5280 —School of Medicine
Georgetown University:
5244 —Undergraduate
5646 —Graduate School
5259 —School of Dentistry
5281 —School of Medicine
5297 Howard University:
5599 —College of Dentistry
5307 —College of Medicine
5610 Johns Hopkins University—Sch. of Advanced Intl. Studies
5422 Mount Vernon College
5622 Southeastern University
5796 Trinity College

FLORIDA

5769 American U. of Caribbean Sch. of Med.
5040 Art Institute of Fort Lauderdale
5053 Barry University
5061 Bethune-Cookman College
5045 Brevard Community College
3709 Briarcliffe College
Broward Community College:
5074 —Fort Lauderdale (Central)
5741 —Hollywood (South)
5735 —Pompano Beach (North)
5127 Central Florida Comm. College
5106 Chipola Junior College
5142 Clearwater Christian College
5437 College of Boca Raton
5173 D.G. Erwin Technical Center
5159 Daytona Beach Community Coll.
5223 Eckerd College
5191 Edison Community College
5182 Edward Waters College
5375 Elinor Smith School
Embry-Riddle Aeronautical University:
5980 —College of Continuing Ed.
5190 —Daytona Beach Campus
5235 Flagler College
5215 Florida A & M University
Florida Atlantic University:
5229 —Boca Raton Campus
5994 —Broward Campus
5216 Florida College
5232 Florida Comm. Coll., Jacksonville
5080 Florida Institute of Technology
3456 Florida Institute of Ultrasound
Florida International University:
5575 —North Miami
5206 —Tamiami Trail
5236 Florida Keys Community College
5217 Florida Memorial College
5218 Florida Southern College
5219 Florida State Univ., Tallahassee
5171 Fort Lauderdale College
5265 Garces Commercial College
5935 George Stone Area Voc. Tech. Center
5271 Gulf Coast Community College
5304 Hillsborough Community College
5327 International Fine Arts College
5337 Jackson Mem. Hosp. Sch. of Nrsg.
5331 Jacksonville University
5377 Lake City Community College
5376 Lake Sumter Community College
5463 Miami Christian College
5920 Miami Institute of Psychology
Miami-Dade Community College:
5624 —Homestead
5465 —Medical Center
5160 —North
5458 —South
5457 —Wolfson
National Education Center:
5712 —Bauder College
5791 —Tampa Tech. Institute
5506 New Coll. of the U. of So. Florida
5162 Northwood Institute
5514 Nova University:
5543 —Law School
5553 Palm Beach Atlantic College
5531 Palm Beach Community College
5562 Pasco Hernando Comm. College
5535 Pensacola Junior College
5548 Polk Community College
5573 Ringling School of Art & Design
Rollins College:
5572 —Day
7744 —Holt Sch./Brevard Campus
5641 Saint John's River Comm. Coll.
5638 Saint Leo College:
5759 —Military Education
5076 Saint Thomas University
5724 —Bilingual Center
5662 Seminole Community College
5666 South Florida Community College
5621 Southeastern College of the Assemblies of God
7131 Southeastern Coll. of Pharm. Sci.
5679 Southern College
5630 Stetson University
5794 Tallahassee Community College
0726 Universidad Central Del Este
5233 University of Central Florida
5812 Univ. of Florida, Gainesville
5175 —College of Dentistry
5803 —College of Medicine
5754 —College of Veterinary Med.
5815 University of Miami
5773 —School of Law

4272 Eastern Idaho Technical College
4355 Idaho State University
4385 Lewis-Clark State College
4539 North Idaho College
4544 Northwest Nazarene College
4657 Ricks College
4843 University of Idaho, Moscow

ILLINOIS

1025 Augustana College
1027 Aurora University
1052 Barat College
1057 Belleville Area College
1483 Black Hawk College, Moline
1065 Blackburn College
1070 Bradley University
1318 Chicago-Kent College of Law
1118 Chicago State University
1083 College of DuPage
1983 College of Lake County
1130 College of Saint Francis
1135 Columbia College
1140 Concordia University
1165 DePaul University
1047 DeVry, Inc.
DeVry Institute of Technology:
Chicago
1171 —Continuing Students
0380 —New/Transfer Students
Lombard
3204 —Continuing Students
0379 —New/Transfer Students
1316 Dr. William M. Scholl College of Podiatric Medicine
1199 Eastern Illinois University
1203 Elgin Community College
1204 Elmhurst College
1206 Eureka College
1263 Governors State University
1256 Greenville College
1089 Harold Washington College
1707 Illinois Benedictine College
1312 Illinois Central College
1315 Illinois College
1318 Illinois Institute of Technology
1319 Illinois State University
1397 Illinois Valley Comm. College
1320 Illinois Wesleyan University
0541 Institute of European/Asian Studies
3235 Introspect Youth Services, Inc.
1344 John Marshall Law School
1346 Joliet Junior College
1351 Judson College
1993 Keller Grad. Sch. of Management
1300 Kendall College
1385 Kishwaukee College
1372 Knox College
1392 Lake Forest College
1404 Lewis University
1406 Lincoln College
1412 Loyola University of Chicago:
1755 —Niles College
1426 —School of Dentistry
1420 —Stritch School of Medicine
1435 MacMurray College
1144 Malcolm X College
1456 McKendree College
1470 Millikin University
1484 Monmouth College
1220 Montay College
1486 Moody Bible Institute
1524 Moraine Valley Community Coll.
1567 National Coll. of Chiropractic
1551 National-Louis University
1555 North Central College
1556 North Park College & Theological Seminary
1090 Northeastern Illinois University
1559 Northern Illinois University
Northwestern University:
3593 —Continuing and Returning Students
3852 —Evening Division
1565 —New Students
1573 Oakton Community College
1596 Olivet Nazarene University
1619 Parkland College
1621 Parks College of St. Louis Univ.
1077 Prairie State College
1630 Principia College
1645 Quincy College
1093 Richard J. Daley College
Robert Morris College:
1662 —Chicago
1717 —Springfield
1674 Rock Valley College
1665 Rockford College
1666 Roosevelt University
1667 Rosary College
3262 Rush Univ.—St. Luke's Med. Ctr.
9626 Saint Anthony Hosp. Sch. of Nrsg.
3033 Saint Augustine College
1747 Saint Francis Hosp. Sch. of Nrsg.
9628 Saint John's Hospital Sch. of Nursing
1708 Saint Xavier College
1713 School of the Art Institute of Chicago
1717 Shimer College
1806 South Suburban College
1726 Southern Illinois Univ. at Carbondale
1759 Southern Illinois Univ. at Edwardsville
1749 State Community College
1820 Trinity Christian College
1810 Trinity College
1821 Triton College
1111 Truman College
1832 University of Chicago—The College (Undergraduate only)
1117 University of Health Sciences, Chicago Medical School
University of Illinois:
1851 —Chicago Circle
1836 —Urbana-Champaign
1938 Waubonsee Community College
1900 Western Illinois University
1905 Wheaton College
1925 Wilbur Wright College
1932 William Rainey Harper College

INDIANA

1015 Ancilla College
1016 Anderson University
1051 Ball State University
1079 Bethel College
1073 Butler University
1776 Calumet College of St. Joseph
1166 DePauw University
1195 Earlham College
1228 Franklin College of Indiana
1251 Goshen College
1252 Grace College & Theological Seminary
1290 Hanover College
1325 Herron School of Art
1309 Holy Cross College
1304 Huntington College
3143 Indiana Business College
1323 Indiana Institute of Technology
1322 Indiana State Univ., Terre Haute
Indiana-Purdue Universities:
1336 —Fort Wayne
1325 —Indianapolis
1361 —School of Dentistry
1285 —School of Medicine
Indiana University:
1324 —Bloomington
7463 —School of Optometry
1338 —Gary
1337 —Kokomo
1314 —New Albany
1194 —Richmond
1339 —South Bend
Indiana Vocational Technical College:
1649 —Anderson
1634 —Bloomington
1286 —Columbus
1277 —Evansville
1278 —Fort Wayne
1281 —Gary
1311 —Indianapolis
1329 —Kokomo
1282 —Lafayette
1334 —Madison
1279 —Muncie
1283 —Richmond
1273 —Sellersburg
1280 —South Bend
1284 —Terre Haute
1647 —Valparaiso
1446 Indiana Wesleyan University
1330 International Business College
1416 Lutheran Coll. of Health Professions
1440 Manchester College
1442 Marian College, Indianapolis
7378 Martin University
1585 Oakland City College
7570 Professional Careers Institute
Purdue University:
1638 —Hammond
1631 —West Lafayette
1640 —Westville
1668 Rose-Hulman Inst. of Technology
1761 Saint Elizabeth Hosp. Sch. of Nrsg.
1693 Saint Francis College
1697 Saint Joseph's College
1704 Saint Mary-of-the-Woods College
1702 Saint Mary's College
1705 Saint Meinrad College
1227 Summit Christian College
1802 Taylor University
1811 Tri-State University
1208 University of Evansville
1321 University of Indianapolis
1841 University of Notre Dame
1335 University of Southern Indiana
1874 Valparaiso University
Vincennes University:
7884 —Jasper
1877 —Vincennes
1895 Wabash College

IOWA

6757 American Institute of Business
6046 Briar Cliff College
6047 Buena Vista College
6087 Central College
6099 Clarke College
6101 Coe College
6119 Cornell College
6177 Des Moines Area Comm. Coll.
6171 Dordt College
6168 Drake University
6193 Ellsworth Community College
1215 Emmaus Bible College
6249 Graceland College
6251 Grand View College
6252 Grinnell College
6289 Hamilton Business College
6288 Hawkeye Inst. of Technology
Indian Hills Community College:
6083 —Centerville
6312 —Ottumwa
6217 Iowa Central Comm. Coll., Ft. Dodge
Iowa Lakes Community College:
6195 —Emmetsburg
6196 —Estherville
6301 Iowa Methodist Hosp. Sch. of Nrsg.
6306 Iowa State University, Ames
6308 Iowa Wesleyan College
Iowa Western Community College:
6098 —Clarinda
6302 —Council Bluffs
6313 Jennie Edmundson Mem. Hosp. Sch.
6027 Kirkwood Community College
6370 Loras College
6375 Luther College
6447 Maharishi International Univ.
6394 Marshalltown Community Coll.
6415 Morningside College
6417 Mount Mercy College
6418 Mount Saint Clare College
6400 North Iowa Area Comm. Coll.
6490 Northwestern College
6593 Palmer College of Chiropractic
6617 Saint Ambrose University
6712 Scott Comm. Coll., Bettendorf
6650 Simpson College, Indianola
Southeastern Community College:
6340 —Keokuk (South)
6048 —West Burlington (North)
6397 Teikyo Marycrest University
6936 Teikyo Westmar University
6869 University of Dubuque
6681 University of Iowa
6307 University of Northern Iowa
6162 Univ. of Osteopathic Medicine & Health Sciences
6885 Upper Iowa University
6094 Vennard College
6925 Waldorf College
6926 Wartburg College
6950 Western Iowa Tech Comm. Coll.
6943 William Penn College

KANSAS

6031 Baker University
6056 Benedictine College
6034 Bethany College
6335 Emporia State University
6262 Haskell Indian Junior College
6334 Kansas State University
6635 Saint Mary of the Plains College
6928 Washburn University
6884 Wichita State University

KENTUCKY

1098 Alice Lloyd College
1019 Asbury College
1023 Ashland Community College
1056 Bellarmine College
1060 Berea College
1071 Brescia College
1097 Campbellsville College
1109 Centre College
1145 Cumberland College
1200 Eastern Kentucky University
1211 Elizabethtown Community Coll.
1249 Georgetown College
1275 Hazard Community College
1307 Henderson Community College
1274 Hopkinsville Community College
8839 Institute of Electronic Tech.
1328 Jefferson Community College
1377 Kentucky Christian College
4161 Kentucky College of Business
1368 Kentucky State University
1369 Kentucky Wesleyan College
1402 Lees College
1474 Lexington Community College
1409 Lindsey Wilson College
1544 Madisonville Community College
1545 Maysville Community College
1532 Mid-Continent Baptist Bible College
1467 Midway College
1487 Morehead State University
1494 Murray State University
1574 Northern Kentucky University:
1574 —Chase Law School
0710 Owensboro Community College
3196 Owensboro Jr. Coll. of Business
1620 Paducah Community College
7579 Phillips College
1625 Pikeville College
1650 Prestonsburg Community Coll.
1690 Saint Catharine College
1779 Somerset Community College
1770 Southeast Community College
1552 Spalding University
1741 Sue Bennett College
3250 Sullivan College
1876 Thomas More College
1808 Transylvania University
1825 Union College
University of Kentucky:
1837 —Lexington
1888 —College of Dentistry
1968 —College of Medicine
1838 University of Louisville:
3814 —School of Dentistry
1967 —School of Medicine
1901 Western Kentucky University

LOUISIANA

0389 **Louisiana State Student Incentive Grant Program**
6082 Centenary College of Louisiana
6176 Delgado Community College
6164 Dillard University
6250 Grambling State University
6662 Jimmy Swaggart Bible College
Louisiana State University:
6373 —Baton Rouge
6385 —New Orleans, Medical Ctr.
6291 —Veterinary Medicine
6372 Louisiana Tech University
6374 Loyola University
6403 McNeese State University
6471 Newcomb Coll. of Tulane Univ.
6482 Northeast Louisiana University
6492 Northwestern State University
6002 Our Lady of Holy Cross College
6656 Southeastern Louisiana Univ.
Southern University:
6663 —Baton Rouge
6711 —New Orleans
6832 Tulane University
6672 Univ. of Southwestern Louisiana
6975 Xavier University of Louisiana

MAINE

3015 Andover College
3074 Bangor Theological Seminary
3076 Bates College
3114 Beal College
3089 Bowdoin College
3269 Bridgton Academy
3700 Casco Bay College
3302 Central Maine Medical Center
3279 Central Maine Tech. College
3280 Colby College
3305 College of the Atlantic
3372 Eastern Maine Tech. College
3440 Husson College
3475 Kennebec Valley Tech. College
3505 Maine Maritime Academy
Mid-State College:
3014 —Auburn
9244 —Augusta
3631 Northern Maine Tech. College
3701 Portland School of Art
3755 Saint Joseph's College
3535 Southern Maine Tech. College
3903 Thomas College
3925 Unity College
University of Maine:
3929 —Augusta
3506 —Farmington
3393 —Fort Kent
3956 —Machias
3916 —Orono
3008 —Presque Isle
3751 University of New England
3923 College of Osteopathic Medicine
3156 Graduate Division
3691 University of Southern Maine
3961 Washington County Tech. College
3960 Westbrook College

MARYLAND

0298 **Maryland State Scholarship Administration**
5028 Allegany Community College
5019 Anne Arundel Community Coll.
5401 Bowie State University
5884 Capitol Bible Sem. Washington Bible College
5101 Capitol College
5137 Catonsville Community College
5144 Charles County Community Coll.
5143 Chesapeake College
5114 Coll. of Notre Dame of Maryland
5890 Columbia Union College
5122 Coppin State College
5176 Dundalk Community College
5192 Essex Community College
5230 Frederick Community College
5402 Frostburg State University
5279 Garrett Community College
5257 Goucher College
5290 Hagerstown Junior College
5303 Harford Community College
5296 Hood College
5308 Howard Community College
Johns Hopkins University:
5332 —Arts and Sciences
5532 —Peabody Institute
5354 —School of Continuing Studies
5353 —School of Engineering
5352 —Sch. of Hygiene & Pub. Health
5767 —School of Nursing
5370 Loyola College
5466 Maryland College of Art & Design
5399 Maryland Inst. College of Art
Montgomery College:
5393 —Germantown
5440 —Rockville
5414 —Takoma Park
5416 Morgan State University
5421 Mount Saint Mary's College
5051 New Comm. Coll. of Baltimore
5545 Prince George's Community Coll.
5598 Saint John's College
5601 Saint Mary's College of Maryland
5403 Salisbury State College
5657 Sojourner Douglas College
5404 Towson State University
5834 Union Mem. Hosp. Sch. of Nrsg.
5810 University of Baltimore
University of Maryland:
5757 —Baltimore City, All Campuses
5835 —Baltimore County
5814 —College Park
5400 —Eastern Shore
0988 —Munich Campus
5804 —University College
5856 Villa Julie College
5888 Washington College
5898 Western Maryland College

MASSACHUSETTS

3002 American International College
3003 Amherst College
3005 Anna Maria College
Aquinas College:
3011 —Milton
3013 —Newton
3777 Art Institute of Boston
3009 Assumption College
3010 Atlantic Union College
3075 Babson College
3078 Bay Path College
3120 Bay State College
3787 Baystate Med. Ctr. Sch. of Nrsg.
Becker College:
3482 —Leicester Campus
3079 —Worcester Campus
3096 Bentley College
3107 Berklee College of Music
3102 Berkshire Community College
8211 Blaine Hair and Beauty Schools
3467 Blue Hills Regional Tech. School
7108 Boston Architectural Center
3060 Boston Business School
3083 Boston College
3084 Boston Conservatory
3813 Boston Technical Center
Boston University:
3087 —All Undergraduates
Graduate Programs:
7100 —Grad. Coll. of Engineering
7423 —Grad. Law School
7485 —Grad. Metropolitan College
3088 —Grad. Programs—Sargent Coll.
3704 —Grad. Sch. for the Arts
3118 —Grad. Sch. of Arts & Sciences
8928 —Grad. Sch. of Dentistry
7148 —Grad. Sch. of Education
7313 —Grad. Sch. of Management
3116 —Grad. Sch. of Medicine
7094 —Grad. Sch. of Nursing
7101 —Grad. Sch. of Public Comm.
8930 —Grad. Sch. of Public Health
3101 —Grad. Sch. of Social Work
3122 —Grad. Sch. of Theology
7098 —Grad. Univ. Professors Prog.
3091 Bradford College
3092 Brandeis University
3026 —Heller Graduate School
3517 Bridgewater State College
3110 Bristol Community College
3112 Brockton Hosp. Sch. of Nrsg.
8213 Broms Academy
3123 Bunker Hill Community College
3099 Burdett School
3097 Butera School of Art
3289 Cape Cod Community College
3279 Clark University
3282 College of the Holy Cross
3285 Curry College
3352 Dean Junior College
8510 Dudley Hall Career Institute
3371 East Coast Aero. Tech. School
3365 Eastern Nazarene College
3283 Elms College
3367 Emerson College
3368 Emmanuel College
3369 Endicott College
3375 Essex Agr. & Tech. Institute
3391 Fisher College, Boston
3518 Fitchburg State College
3392 Forsyth Sch. for Dent. Hygienists
5802 —School of Medicine
5490 University of North Florida
5828 University of South Florida
5819 University of Tampa
5833 University of West Florida
5869 Valencia Community College
9807 Ward Stone College
5893 Webber College

GEORGIA

5001 Abraham Baldwin Agri. College
5002 Agnes Scott College
5004 Albany State College
5042 American Coll. for Applied Arts
5009 Andrew College
5012 Armstrong State College
5429 Art Institute of Atlanta
5737 Athens Area Tech. Institute
5030 Atlanta Area Technical School
5029 Atlanta Christian College
5014 Atlanta College of Art
5725 Atlanta Metropolitan College
5336 Augusta College
5713 Augusta Technical Institute
5062 Bainbridge College
5070 Bauder College
5059 Berry College
5066 Brenau College
5068 Brewton-Parker College
5078 Brunswick College
5110 Clark Atlanta University
5145 Clayton State College
5123 Columbus College
6124 Covenant College
5167 Dalton College
5026 Darton College
5165 DeKalb College
5693 DeKalb Technical Institute
DeVry Institute of Technology:
5715 —Continuing Students
0371 —New/Transfer Students
5200 East Georgia College
5184 Emmanuel College
5187 Emory University
5237 Floyd College
5220 Fort Valley State College
5273 Gainesville College
5777 Georgia Baptist Coll. of Nursing
5252 Georgia College
5248 Georgia Institute of Technology
5249 Georgia Military College
5253 Georgia Southern University
5250 Georgia Southwestern College
5251 Georgia State Univ. Atlanta:
5283 —College of Law
5256 Gordon College
5263 Grady Mem. Hosp. Sch. of Rad. Tech.
5168 Gwinnett Technical Institute
5384 Interdenominational Theological Seminary
5359 Kennesaw State College
5362 LaGrange College
5487 Lane School of Art
7578 Life College
5439 Macon College
5406 Medical College of Georgia
Mercer University:
5025 —Atlanta
5409 —Macon
5983 —School of Law
5471 —School of Medicine
5623 —Southern School of Pharmacy
5523 —University College
5411 Middle Georgia College
5415 Morehouse College
8277 Morehouse School of Medicine
5417 Morris Brown College
5497 North Georgia College
5507 North Georgia Tech. & Voc. Sch.
5521 Oglethorpe University
5186 Oxford College
5530 Paine College
5537 Piedmont College
5568 Reinhardt College
5636 Savannah Area Voc. Tech. School
5631 Savannah College of Art & Design
5609 Savannah State College
5616 Shorter College
5619 South Georgia College
5626 Southern College of Tech.
5628 Spelman College
5784 Thomas Technical Institute
5799 Toccoa Falls College
5798 Truett McConnell College
5813 University of Georgia, Athens
5855 Valdosta State College
5889 Waycross College
5895 Wesleyan College
5900 West Georgia College
5786 West Georgia Technical Institute
5990 Young Harris College

HAWAII

4106 Brigham Young University
4324 Cannon's International Business Coll.
4105 Chaminade Univ. of Honolulu
9964 Forest Inst. of Professional Psych.
0545 Hawaii Community Foundation
4351 Hawaii Loa College
4352 Hawaii Pacific University
0417 Kamehameha School
University of Hawaii:
4869 —Hilo
4350 —Honolulu Community College
4377 —Kapiolani Community College
4378 —Kauai Community College
4410 —Leeward Community College
4867 —Manoa
4510 —Maui Community College
4959 —West Oahu
4976 —Windward Community College

IDAHO

3319 Boise Bible College
4018 Boise State University
4060 College of Idaho
4114. College of Southern Idaho

3519 Framingham State College
3394 Franklin Institute of Boston
3417 Gordon College
3420 Greenfield Community College
3447 Hampshire College
Harvard University
3434 —Harvard-Radcliffe College
3380 —Continuing Education
3455 —Grad. School of Design
3428 —Grad. School of Education
3458 —J. F. Kennedy Sch. of Gov't
3457 —Law School
3450 —Medical School
3038 —School of Public Health
3449 Hellenic College
7412 Hickox School
3437 Holyoke Community College
8841 ITT Technical Institute
3473 Katharine Gibbs School
3696 Kinyon Campbell Business School
3287 Laboure College
3481 Lasell College
3488 Lawrence Mem. Hosp. Sch. of Nrsg.
8993 Learning Institute for Beauty Sciences
3483 Lesley College
8994 Lowell Academy
Mansfield Beauty Schools:
9097 —Quincy Campus
9099 —Springfield Campus
9100 Marian Court Junior College
3294 Mass. Bay Comm. College
3516 Mass. College of Art
3512 Mass. Coll. of Pharm. & Allied Health
3514 Mass. Institute of Tech.
3515 Mass. Maritime Academy
3474 Mass. Sch. of Prof. Psychology
3549 Massasoit Community College
3525 Merrimack College
3554 Middlesex Community College
9101 Montserrat College of Art
3529 Mount Holyoke College
3530 Mount Ida College
3545 Mount Wachusett Comm. College
3676 New England Baptist Hosp. School of Nursing
3659 New England Conserv. of Music
3645 New England Sch. of Art & Design
3288 New England School of Law
9347 New England Sch. of Photography
3639 Newbury College
3666 Nichols College
3521 North Adams State College
9270 North Bennet Street Schools
3651 North Shore Community College
3641 Northeast Inst. of Indust. Tech.
3667 Northeastern University
3674 Northern Essex Community Coll.
3689 Pine Manor College
3713 Quincy Junior College
3714 Quinsigamond Community College
3723 Regis College
3322 Rob Roy Academy
3740 Roxbury Community College
3773 Saint Elizabeth's Hosp. Sch. of Nrsg.
3756 Saint John's School of Business
3295 Saint John's Seminary College
3522 Salem State College
3764 Salter School
3794 Sch. of the Museum of Fine Arts
3761 Simmons College
3795 Simon's Rock College of Bard
3762 Smith College
3799 Somerville Hosp. Sch. of Nrsg.
3786 Southeastern Mass. Univ.
3763 Springfield College
3791 Springfield Tech. Comm. College
3770 Stonehill College
3771 Suffolk University
3039 Travel School of America
Tufts University:
3901 —Tufts/Jackson
8158 —Dental Medicine (Grad only)
3399 —Fletcher School (Grad only)
3896 —Medical School (Grad only)
3893 —Veterinary Medicine (Grad only)
3901 —All other applicants
3911 University of Lowell
University of Massachusetts:
3917 —Amherst
3924 —Boston
3936 —Medical School
3957 Wellesley College
3958 Wentworth Inst. of Technology
3812 Wentworth Technical School
3962 Western New England College
3523 Westfield State College
3963 Wheaton College
3964 Wheelock College
3965 Williams College
3969 Worcester Polytechnic Institute
3524 Worcester State College
3976 Worcester Technical Institute
3970 Youville Hosp. Sch. of Nursing

MICHIGAN

1001 Adrian College
1007 Albion College
1010 Alma College
1011 Alpena Community College
1030 Andrews University
1018 Aquinas College
3851 Argubright Business College
Baker College:
3237 —Flint
1616 —Mount Clemens
1527 —Muskegon
3299 —Owosso
1618 —Pontiac
1617 —Port Huron
1049 Bay de Noc Community College
1095 Calvin College
1035 Center for Creative Studies
1106 Central Michigan University
1225 Charles Stewart Mott Comm. Coll.
1123 Cleary College
1094 Concordia College
1156 Cranbrook Academy of Art
Davenport College of Business:
1183 —Grand Rapids
7490 —Kalamazoo
7235 —Lansing
1816 Delta College
1767 D'Etre University
Detroit College of Business:
1181 —Dearborn
1190 —Flint
1158 —Warren
1168 Detroit College of Law
1201 Eastern Michigan University
1222 Ferris State University
1261 Glen Oaks Community College
1246 GMI Engineering & Mgmt. Inst.
1250 Gogebic Community College
1265 Grace Bible College
1253 Grand Rapids Baptist Coll. & Sem.
1254 Grand Rapids Junior College
8706 Grand Rapids Sch. Bible & Music
1258 Grand Valley State University
3238 Great Lakes Junior College
1293 Henry Ford Community College
1294 Highland Park Community College
1295 Hillsdale College
1301 Hope College
1340 Jackson Community College
1952 Jordan College
1365 Kalamazoo College
1378 Kalamazoo Valley Comm. College
1375 Kellogg Community College
1376 Kendall College of Art & Design
1382 Kirtland Community College
4200 Krainz-Woods Acad. Med. Lab. Technicians
1137 Lake Michigan College
1421 Lake Superior State University
1414 Lansing Community College
1399 Lawrence Technological Univ.
1425 Lewis College of Business
1722 Macomb Community College
1437 Madonna University
1452 Marygrove College
1465 Michigan State University
1464 Michigan Technological Univ.
1523 Mid-Michigan Community Coll.
1514 Monroe County Comm. College
1522 Montcalm Community College
1495 Muskegon Community College
1569 North Central Michigan College
1560 Northern Michigan University
1564 Northwestern Michigan College
1568 Northwood Institute
Oakland Community College:
3706 —Auburn Hills
3708 —Highland Lakes
3707 —Orchard Ridge
7267 —Southeast
1497 Oakland University
1595 Olivet College
1672 Reformed Bible College
1766 Saginaw Valley State Univ.
1628 Saint Clair County Comm. Coll.
1753 Saint Mary's College
1764 Schoolcraft College
1719 Siena Heights College
1783 Southwestern Michigan College
1732 Spring Arbor College
1743 Suomi College
1796 Thomas M. Cooley Law School
1835 University of Detroit Mercy
University of Michigan:
1839 —Ann Arbor
5848 —School of Dentistry
6018 —School of Public Health
6050 —School of Social Work
1861 —Dearborn
1853 —Flint
1894 Walsh Coll. of Accounting & Business Administration
1935 Washtenaw Community College
1937 Wayne County Community Coll.
Wayne State University:
1268 —Graduate School
1114 —Law School
1949 —Medical School
1898 —Undergraduate
1941 West Shore Community College
1902 Western Michigan University
1167 William Tyndale College

MINNESOTA

6014 Augsburg College
6676 Bemidji State University
6035 Bethany Lutheran College
6038 Bethel College
6081 Carleton College
6104 College of Saint Benedict
6105 College of Saint Catherine
6107 College of Saint Scholastica
6113 Concordia College, Moorhead
6114 Concordia College, St. Paul
6435 Dr. Martin Luther College
6253 Gustavus Adolphus College
6265 Hamline University
6390 Macalester College
6411 Minneapolis Coll. of Art & Design
6678 Moorhead State University
6505 North Central Bible College
6489 Northwestern College
6516 Northwestern Coll. of Chiropractic
6679 Saint Cloud State University
7828 Saint John's Preparatory School
6624 Saint John's University
6632 Saint Mary's College
6638 Saint Olaf College
6110 University of Saint Thomas

MISSISSIPPI

0320 State Inst. of Higher Learning Board of Trustees, Jackson
1008 Alcorn State University
1055 Belhaven College
1066 Blue Mountain College
1122 Clarke College
1126 Coahoma Community College
1142 Copiah-Lincoln Junior College
1163 Delta State University
1296 Hinds Community College
1299 Holmes Junior College
1341 Jackson State University
1347 Jones County Junior College
1471 Millsaps College
Mississippi College:
1477 —Clinton Campus
1478 —MC-Clarke Campus
1455 —MC-School of Law
1742 Mississippi Delta Comm. College
1480 Mississippi State University
1481 Mississippi Univ. for Women
1482 Mississippi Valley State Univ.
1557 Northeast Mississippi Comm. Coll.
1562 Northwest Mississippi Comm. Coll.
1669 Rust College
1807 Tougaloo College
University of Mississippi:
1879 —Medical Center
1840 —Oxford/University
1479 Univ. of Southern Mississippi, Hattiesburg
1858 Utica Junior College
1923 Wesley College
1907 William Carey College

MISSOURI

6085 Central Bible College
6089 Central Methodist College
6090 Central Missouri State University
6095 Columbia College
6123 Culver-Stockton College
DeVry Institute of Technology:
6092 —Continuing Students
0347 —New Students
6169 Drury College
6198 Evangel College
6216 Fontbonne College
6269 Harris-Stowe State College
6330 Kansas City Art Institute
6366 Lincoln University
6367 Lindenwood College
6352 Logan College of Chiropractic
6399 Maryville College
6413 Missouri Valley College
6625 Missouri Western State College
6483 Northeast Missouri State Univ.
6488 Northwest Missouri State Univ.
6574 Park College
6611 Rockhurst College
6626 Saint Louis College of Pharmacy
Saint Louis Community College:
6225 —Florissant Valley
6226 —Forest Park
6430 —Meramec
6629 Saint Louis University:
6720 —School of Medicine
6655 Southeast Missouri State Univ.
6665 Southwest Missouri State Univ.
6683 Stephens College
University of Missouri:
6875 —Columbia
6872 —Kansas City
6889 —St. Louis
6929 Washington University:
6952 —School of Medicine
6955 —Health Administration
6956 —Nurse Anesthesia
6958 —Occupational Therapy
6959 —Physical Therapy
6933 Webster University
6937 Westminster College
6941 William Jewell College
6944 William Woods College

MONTANA

4041 Carroll College
4058 College of Great Falls
4280 Dawson Community College
4298 Eastern Montana College
4317 Flathead Valley Community Coll.
4811 Fort Belknap College
4081 Miles Community College
4487 Montana College of Mineral Science & Technology
4488 Montana State Univ., Bozeman
4538 Northern Montana College
4660 Rocky Mountain College
4489 University of Montana, Missoula
4945 Western Montana College

NEBRASKA

6053 Bellevue College
6066 Bishop Clarkson College
6058 Bryan Memorial Hosp. Sch. of Nrsg.
Central Community College:
6584 —Columbus
6346 —Grand Island
6136 —Hastings
6466 Chadron State College
6106 College of Saint Mary
6116 Concordia Teachers College
6121 Creighton University:
7177 —School of Dentistry
7220 —School of Law
8139 —School of Medicine
7221 —School of Pharmacy
6157 Dana College
6165 Doane College
6270 Hastings College
6401 McCook Community College
6458 Metropolitan Comm. College
6406 Midland Lutheran College
6503 Nebraska Christian College
6886 Nebraska Coll. of Tech. Agriculture
6470 Nebraska Wesleyan University
6473 Northeast Tech. Comm. College
6468 Peru State College
Southeast Community College:
6491 —Beatrice
6349 —Lincoln
6502 —Milford
University of Nebraska:
6467 —Kearney
6877 —Lincoln
6896 —Medical Center
6420 —Omaha
6469 Wayne State College

NEVADA

4757 Sierra Nevada College
4960 Truckee Meadows Comm. College
University of Nevada:
4861 —Las Vegas
4844 —Reno
4972 Western Nevada Comm. College

NEW HAMPSHIRE

3694 Antioch Univ. New England
3310 Castle Junior College
3281 Colby-Sawyer College
3648 Daniel Webster College
3351 Dartmouth College
3395 Franklin Pierce College
3452 Hesser College, Manchester
3472 Keene State College
3657 New England College
3649 New Hampshire College
New Hampshire Technical College:
3646 —Berlin
3684 —Claremont
3683 —Laconia
3660 —Manchester
3643 —Nashua
3661 —Stratham
3647 New Hampshire Technical Inst.
3670 Notre Dame College
3690 Plymouth State College
3728 Rivier College
3748 Saint Anselm College
3918 University of New Hampshire:
3912 —Manchester
3977 White Pines College

NEW JERSEY

2268 Ann May School of Nursing
2024 Atlantic Community College
2032 Bergen Community College
2838 Bergen County Tech. Inst.
2061 Berkeley Coll. of Bus., Garret Mt.
2044 Bloomfield College
2181 Brookdale Community College
2180 Burlington County College
2072 Caldwell College
2121 Camden County College
2080 Centenary College
2090 College of Saint Elizabeth
2124 County College of Morris
2118 Cumberland County College
DeVry Technical Institute:
2203 —Continuing Students
0341 —New/Transfer Students
2193 Drew University
2239 Elizabeth Gen. Med. Ctr. Sch. of Nrsg.
2237 Essex County College
Fairleigh Dickinson University:
2232 —Edward Williams College
2262 —Madison
2255 —Rutherford
2263 —Teaneck
2321 Felician College
2274 Georgian Court College
2515 Glassboro State College
2281 Gloucester County College
2304 Holy Name Hosp. Sch. of Nrsg.
2291 Hudson County Community Coll.
2516 Jersey City State College
8937 Katharine Gibbs Sch., Montclair
2517 Kean College of New Jersey
2444 Mercer County Community Coll.
2441 Middlesex County College
2416 Monmouth College
2520 Montclair State College
2427 Mountainside Hosp. Sch. of Nrsg.
2452 Muhlenburg Regional Medical Ctr.
2513 New Jersey Inst. of Technology
2630 Ocean County College
2694 Passaic Co. Community College
2672 Princeton University
2884 Ramapo College of New Jersey
2867 Raritan Valley Comm. College
2758 Rider College
Rutgers The State University:
2737 —ALL New Brunswick Colleges
2092 —Camden Coll. of Arts and Sci.
2512 —Newark College of Arts and Sciences and Nursing
2875 Saint Francis Comm. Health Ctr., School of Nursing
2806 Saint Peter's College
2868 Salem Community College
2811 Seton Hall University:
2826 —School of Law
2819 Stevens Institute of Technology
2889 Stockton State College
2711 Sussex County Community College
2911 Teterboro Sch. of Aeronautics
2748 Thomas Edison State College
2519 Trenton State College
2921 Union County College
2578 Univ. of Medicine & Dentistry of N.J., Newark
2930 Upsala College
2722 Warren County Community College
2974 Westminster Choir College
2518 William Paterson College of N.J.

NEW MEXICO

4220 Albuquerque Tech. Voc. School
4290 Clovis Comm. College
4676 College of Santa Fe
4116 College of the Southwest
Eastern New Mexico University:
4299 —Portales
4662 —Roswell
7469 Institute of American Indian Arts
4422 Luna Voc. Tech. School
4532 New Mexico Highlands Univ.
4533 New Mexico Institute of Mining & Tech.
4553 New Mexico Junior College
4534 New Mexico Military Institute
New Mexico State University:
4012 —Alamogordo
4547 —Carlsbad
4781 —Dona Ana Branch Comm. Coll.
4552 —Grants
4531 —Las Cruces
4560 Northern New Mexico Comm. Coll.
4737 Saint John's College
4732 San Juan College
4816 Santa Fe Community College
9842 Southwestern Indian Polytechnic Institute
University of New Mexico:
4845 —Albuquerque
4895 —Gallup
4809 —Los Alamos
4889 —School of Medicine
4810 —Valencia County
4535 Western New Mexico University

NEW YORK

2003 Adelphi University
2017 Adirondack Community College
2013 Albany College of Pharmacy
2522 Alfred State College
2005 Alfred University
2060 —SUNY College of Ceramics
2603 American Acad. of Dramatic Arts
2498 American Musical and Dramatic Academy
2016 Arnot-Ogden Mem. Hosp. Sch. of Nrsg.
2037 Bard College
2038 Barnard College
3407 Bayley Seton Hosp. Physician Asst. Training Program
2064 Berkeley College
3339 BOCES Cattaraugus — Allegany School of Practical Nursing
5817 BOCES Rensselaer — School of Practical Nursing
7983 BOCES Steuben — Allegany College of Practical Nursing
2901 Boricua College
Briarcliffe School:
2605 —Hicksville
7107 —Lynbrook
8275 —Patchogue
8343 —Evening Div.—All Campuses
2048 Broome Community College
Bryant & Stratton Business Institute:
2018 —Albany
2058 —Buffalo
8239 —Rochester
2720 Bryant & Stratton Powelson Business Institute
2073 Canisius College
2010 Cayuga County Community Coll.
2078 Cazenovia College
2390 Circle in the Square Theatre Sch.
Clarkson University:
2084 —Continuing and Returning Students
0707 —New Freshmen
2266 —New Transfers
2315 —The Clarkson School
2135 Clinton Community College
2086 Colgate University
2001 College of Aeronautics
2112 College of Insurance
2088 College of Mount Saint Vincent
College of New Rochelle:
7193 —Graduate
7192 —New Resources
7191 —School of Nursing
2089 —Undergraduate
2091 College of Saint Rose
Columbia University:
2116 —Columbia College
2120 —Graduate Sch. of Journalism
2094 —Sch. of Dental & Oral Surgery
2111 —School of Engr. and Applied Sci.
2095 —School of General Studies
2142 —School of Nursing
2905 —Teachers College
2138 Columbia-Greene Comm. Coll.
2134 Community Coll. of the Finger Lakes
2096 Concordia College
2097 Cooper Union
Cornell University:
2098 —Endowed
2110 —Statutory
2106 Corning Community College
6787 Council on Intl. Ed. Exchange
2109 Crouse-Irving Mem. Hosp. Sch. of Nrsg.
3301 Culinary Institute of America
2762 Daemen College
2190 Dominican College of Blauvelt
2011 Dowling College
2198 Dutchess Community College
2197 D'Youville College
2224 Eastman School of Music
2226 Elmira College
Erie Community College:
2213 —City Campus
2228 —North Campus
2211 —South Campus
2257 Fashion Institute of Technology
3142 Five Towns College
Fordham University:
3031 —Lincoln Center Campus
2259 —Rose Hill Campus
2248 Friends World College
2254 Fulton-Montgomery Comm. Coll.
2272 Genesee Community College
8775 Grumman Data Systems Institute
2286 Hamilton College
2288 Hartwick College
2316 Herkimer County Comm. College
2334 Hilbert College
2294 Hobart College
2295 Hofstra University
2299 Houghton College
2300 Hudson Valley Community Coll.
Iona College:
2324 —All Day & General Studies
9931 —All Weekend, Evening & Nursing
2325 Ithaca College
2335 Jamestown Community College
2345 Jefferson Community College
2339 Jewish Theol. Sem. of America
2340 Juilliard School
2350 Keuka College
2352 King's College
2380 Laboratory Institute of Mdse.
2366 Le Moyne College
2502 Long Island Beauty School
2377 Long Island Coll. Hosp. Sch. of Nursg.
Long Island University:
2369 —Brooklyn
2070 —C.W. Post Campus, Brookville
2604 —C.W. Post Center, Brentwood
2853 —Southampton
2395 Manhattan College, Riverdale
2396 Manhattan School of Music
2397 Manhattanville College, Purchase
2398 Mannes College of Music
Maria College of Albany:
2434 —Day
2564 —Evening and Weekend
7714 Marion S. Whelan School of Practical Nursing
2400 Marist College

6361 Langston University
6257 Mid-America Bible College
6484 Northeastern Oklahoma A & M Coll
6485 Northeastern State University
6543 Oklahoma City University
6557 Oklahoma Jr. Coll. of Bus. and Tech
Oral Roberts University:
7492 —Graduate School
7493 —Medical School
6552 —Undergraduate Division
6579 Phillips University
6559 Rose State College
6036 Southern Nazarene University
6673 Southwestern Oklahoma St. Univ
6749 Spartan School of Aeronautics
6839 Tulsa Junior College
6091 Univ. of Central Oklahoma
6879 Univ. of Oklahoma, Norman
6902 —Health Science Center
6883 University of Tulsa

OREGON

8104 A Art College of Beauty
4231 Bassist College
8253 Beau Monde College of Hair Design
4025 Blue Mountain Comm. College
4090 Central Oregon Comm. College
4745 Chemeketa Community College
4111 Clackamas Community College
4089 Clatsop Community College
7433 College of Legal Arts
4093 Columbia Christian College
4079 Concordia College
4300 Eastern Oregon State College
4274 Eugene Bible College
4325 George Fox College
4407 Lane Community College
4384 Lewis and Clark College
4387 Linfield College:
4333 —Linfield-Good Samaritan, Nursing
4413 Linn-Benton Community College
4480 Marylhurst College
4508 Mount Hood Community College
4496 Multnomah School of the Bible
4543 Northwest Christian College
9377 Oregon City Beauty School
8985 Oregon Coll. of Beauty & Barbering
4900 Oregon Health Sciences University
4587 Oregon Institute of Technology:
4667 —Metro Campus (Portland)
4586 Oregon State University
4504 Pacific Northwest Coll. of Art
4601 Pacific University
7708 Phagans Central Oregon Bty. Coll.
7706 Phagans School of Beauty
4617 Portland Community College
4610 Portland State University
4654 Reed College
4653 Rogue Community College
4702 Southern Oregon State College
4729 Southwestern Oregon Comm. Coll.
9767 Springfield College of Beauty
4825 Treasure Valley Comm. College
4862 Umpqua Community College
4846 University of Oregon
4847 University of Portland
4595 Warner Pacific College
4956 Western Baptist College
4980 Western Business College
4968 Western Conservative Baptist Seminary
4585 Western Oregon State College
4979 Western States Chiroprac. Coll.
4954 Willamette University

PENNSYLVANIA

2004 Albright College
2006 Allegheny College
2021 Allentown College of Saint Francis de Sales
2431 Alvernia College
8117 Art Institute of Philadelphia
2029 Art Institute of Pittsburgh
2036 Baptist Bible College & Seminary
2039 Beaver College
2049 Bryn Mawr College
2050 Bucknell University
2066 Bucks County Community Coll.
2071 Cabrini College
2647 California University of Pa.
2421 Carlow College
2074 Carnegie Mellon University
2079 Cedar Crest College
2081 Chatham College
2082 Chestnut Hill College
2648 Cheyney University of Pa.
2649 Clarion University of Pa.
2087 College Misericordia
Community College of Allegheny County:
2156 —Allegheny County Campus
2122 —Boyce Campus
2025 —College Center North
2123 —South Campus
2682 Community Coll. of Philadelphia
2100 Curtis Institute of Music
2125 Delaware County Comm. College
2186 Dickinson College
2194 Drexel University
2196 Duquesne University
2650 East Stroudsburg Univ. of Pa.
2704 Eastern Baptist Theological Seminary
2220 Eastern College
2651 Edinboro University of Pa.
2225 Elizabethtown College
2261 Franklin and Marshall College
2270 Gannon University
2273 Geneva College
2275 Gettysburg College
2277 Grove City College
2278 Gwynedd-Mercy College
Hahnemann University:
2285 —Graduate School
2306 —School of Health Sciences
2287 Harcum Junior College
2309 Harrisburg Area Comm. College
2289 Haverford College
2297 Holy Family College
2320 Immaculata College
2341 Juniata College
2351 Keystone Junior College
2353 King's College
2653 Kutztown University of Pa.
2379 La Roche College
2363 La Salle University
2361 Lafayette College
2364 Lebanon Valley College
2365 Lehigh University
2367 Lincoln Univ. of the Comm. of Pa.
2654 Lock Haven University of Pa.
2382 Luzerne County Comm. College
2372 Lycoming College
2655 Mansfield University of Pa.
2407 Marywood College
2410 Mercyhurst College
2411 Messiah College
2458 Methodist Hospital
2656 Millersville University of Pa.
2445 Montgomery Co. Community Coll.
2417 Moore College of Art and Design
2418 Moravian College
2423 Muhlenberg College
2628 Neumann College
2567 Northeastern Christian Jr. College
2573 Northampton Co. Area Comm. Coll.
8662 Pennsylvania College of Straight Chiropractic
9266 Pennsylvania School of Art & Design
2660 Pennsylvania State University (All Campuses)
2661 Philadelphia College of Bible
2663 Phila. Coll. of Pharmacy & Sci.
2666 Phila. Coll. of Textiles & Science
2674 Pierce Junior College
2718 Pinebrook Junior College
2676 Point Park College
2769 Robert Morris College
2763 Rosemont College
2797 Saint Francis College
2801 Saint Joseph's University
2808 Saint Vincent College
2812 Seton Hill College
2657 Shippensburg University of Pa.
2658 Slippery Rock University of Pa.
2817 Spring Garden College
2820 Susquehanna University
2821 Swarthmore College
Temple University:
9917 —Allied Health
2643 —Ambler
2917 —Dental, Medical, & Pharmacy
9940 —Graduate
7876 —Law
2912 —Tyler School of Art
2906 —Undergraduate
2910 Thiel College
2903 Thomas Jefferson University, Coll. of Allied Health Sciences
2926 University of Pennsylvania
University of Pittsburgh:
2935 —Bradford
2865 —College Work Study
2936 —Greensburg
2934 —Johnstown
2927 —Pittsburgh
2949 —School of Medicine
7466 —Semester at Sea
2937 —Titusville
2929 University of Scranton
2664 University of the Arts
2931 Ursinus College
2579 Valley Forge Christian College
2955 Valley Forge Military Jr. College
2959 Villanova University
2967 Washington and Jefferson Coll.
2969 Waynesburg College
2975 Westminster College
2642 Widener University
2977 Wilkes University
2979 Wilson College
2991 York College of Pennsylvania

RHODE ISLAND

7053 Arthur Angelo School of Hair Design
Brown University:
3094 —Continuing Undergraduates only
3189 —New Freshmen & Transfers only
3095 Bryant College
Community College of Rhode Island:
3738 —Lincoln
3733 —Warwick
3465 Johnson and Wales University
3476 Katharine Gibbs School
9315 New England Inst. Tech. of R.I.
7882 Ocean State Business Institute
3693 Providence College
3724 Rhode Island College
3726 Rhode Island School of Design
7733 Rhode Island School of Photography
3729 Roger Williams College
3759 Salve Regina University
Sawyer School:
9829 —Pawtucket
7329 —Warwick
7774 School of Medical Sec. Sciences
3919 University of Rhode Island
3954 Warwick Acad. of Beauty Culture

SOUTH CAROLINA

0187 **South Carolina Tuition Grants Agency**
5037 Aiken Technical College
5008 Anderson College
5056 Benedict College
5065 Bob Jones University
5896 Central Wesleyan College
5079 Charleston Southern University
5095 Chesterfield-Marlboro Tech. Coll.
5108 Citadel, The
5109 Claflin College
5111 Clemson University
5112 Coker College
5113 College of Charleston
5117 Columbia College
5121 Converse College
5744 Denmark Tech. College
5188 Erskine College
5207 Florence-Darlington Tech. Coll.
5442 Francis Marion College
5222 Furman University
5278 Greenville Technical College
5305 Horry-Georgetown Tech. College
5456 Johnson & Wales University
5363 Lander College
5366 Limestone College
5584 Midlands Technical College
5418 Morris College
2406 Marymount College, Tarrytown:
9812 —Weekend Program
2405 Marymount Manhattan College
2436 Mater Dei College
2422 Medaille College
2472 Memorial Hospital Sch. of Nursing
2409 Mercy College
Millard Fillmore Hospital:
9779 —Radiology Technicians School
2456 —Registered Nursing School
2414 Mohawk Valley Community Coll.
2415 Molloy College
Monroe College:
2463 —Bronx
2465 —New Rochelle
2429 Monroe Community College
2423 Mount Saint Mary College
2455 Mount Vernon Hosp. Sch. Nursing
2559 National Shakespeare Company Conservatory
2511 Nazareth College of Rochester
New School for Social Research:
2521 —Graduate
9384 —Undergraduate
2169 New York Chiropractic College
2550 New York City Tech. College (Both Campuses)
2561 New York Inst. of Technology (All Campuses)
2552 New York Law School
9297 New York Sch. of Interior Design
New York University:
2562 —Undergraduate & Grad. Schools
2581 —Graduate School of Medicine
2489 —Allied Health Education
2568 Niagara County Community Coll.
2558 Niagara University
2571 North Country Community Coll.
2560 Nyack College
2623 Olean Business Institute
2627 Onondaga Community College
2625 Orange County Community Coll.
Pace University:
2635 —Undergraduate, New York City
2685 —Undergraduate, Pleasantville
2276 —Undergraduate, White Plains
2844 —School of Law, White Plains
2478 —Graduate, New York City
2546 —Graduate, Pleasantville
2644 —Graduate, White Plains
2638 Parsons School of Design
2640 Paul Smith's Coll. of Arts & Sci.
2031 Phillips Beth Israel Med. Ctr. School of Nursing
Polytechnic University:
2668 —Brooklyn
2695 —Farmingdale (not SUNY—Farmingdale)
2669 Pratt Institute
2757 Rensselaer Polytechnic Institute
2759 Roberts Wesleyan College
2760 Rochester Inst. of Technology:
9926 —Natl. Tech. Inst. for the Deaf
9549 Rochester Sch. of Practical Nrsg.
2767 Rockland Community College
Ross University:
2020 —Sch. of Medicine
2305 —Sch. of Veterinary Med.
2764 Russell Sage College
2343 Sage Jr. Coll. of Albany
2793 Saint Bonaventure University
Saint Elizabeth Hospital:
2847 —School of Nursing
4192 —School of Radiography
2796 Saint Francis College
7762 Saint George Univ. Sch. of Med.
2798 Saint John Fisher College
2894 Saint John's Riverside Hosp., Cochran School of Nursing
2799 Saint John's University
Saint Joseph's College:
2802 —Brooklyn
2841 —Patchogue
2825 Saint Joseph's Hosp. Health Ctr.
2805 Saint Lawrence University
9741 Saint Luke's Memorial Hospital Ctr. Diagnostic Radiography
2807 Saint Thomas Aquinas College
2749 Saint Vincent's School of Nursing
9732 Samaritan Hospital Sch. of Nrsg.
2810 Sarah Lawrence College
2879 Schenectady Co. Comm. College
2835 School of Visual Arts
2814 Siena College
2837 Sisters of Charity Hosp. Sch. of Nrsg.
2815 Skidmore College
State University of New York:
2524 —Agr. & Tech. College at Cobleskill
2527 —Agr. & Tech. Coll. at Morrisville
2532 —Center at Albany
2535 —Center at Binghamton
2925 —Center at Buffalo/Amherst
2925 —Health Science Center
2548 —Center at Stony Brook
2891 —Health Science Center
7461 —Sch. of Dental Medicine
7462 —Sch. of Medicine
2537 —College at Brockport
2533 —College at Buffalo
2538 —College at Cortland
2539 —College at Fredonia
2540 —College at Geneseo
2541 —College at New Paltz
2866 —College at Old Westbury
2542 —College at Oneonta
2543 —College at Oswego
2544 —College at Plattsburgh
2545 —College at Potsdam
2878 —College at Purchase
2530 —College of Environmental Science & Forestry
2522 —College of Technology at Alfred
2523 —College of Technology at Canton
2525 —College of Technology at Delhi
2526 —College of Tech. at Farmingdale
2214 —Empire State College
2534 —Health Science Center at Brooklyn
2547 —Health Science Center at Syracuse
2896 —Institute of Tech. at Utica/Rome
2536 —Maritime College
8319 Stenotype Academy
8860 —Evening Division
Suffolk County Community College:
2849 —Brentwood, Western Campus
2846 —Riverhead, Eastern Campus
2827 —Selden, Ammerman Campus
2855 Sullivan County Comm. College
2823 Syracuse University:
7833 —College of Law
2913 Tobe-Coburn Sch. for Fashion Careers
2904 Tompkins-Cortland Comm. Coll.
2902 Touro College
2856 Trocaire College
2938 Ulster County Community Coll.
2920 Union College & University
2922 Union Theological Seminary
2067 United States Merchant Marine Academy
2928 University of Rochester
2932 Utica College of Syracuse Univ.
2956 Vassar College
2962 Villa Maria College
4152 Vocational Ed. & Extension Bd.
2966 Wagner College
2971 Wells College
2972 Westchester Community College
2978 William Smith College
7974 Word of Life Bible Institute
2765 Yeshiva Chofetz Chaim Radin
Yeshiva University:
2990 —Undergraduate Division
2960 —Benjamin Cardozo Sch. of Law
2551 —Ferkauf Grad. Sch. of Psych.
2980 —Wurzweiler Sch. of Social Work

NORTH CAROLINA

5010 Appalachian State University
5052 Barber-Scotia College
5016 Barton College
5055 Belmont Abbey College
5058 Bennett College
5043 Blue Ridge Community College
5067 Brevard College
5300 Brunswick Community College
5100 Campbell University
5094 Cape Fear Community College
5103 Catawba College
5102 Central Piedmont Comm. College
5107 Chowan College
5134 Coastal Carolina Comm. College
5133 College of the Albemarle
5150 Davidson College
5156 Duke University:
5152 —School of Medicine
5180 East Carolina University:
5721 —School of Medicine
5629 Elizabeth City State University
5183 Elon College
5212 Fayetteville State University
5234 Forsyth Technical College
5242 Gardner-Webb College
5262 Gaston College
5260 Greensboro College
5261 Guilford College
5275 Guilford Technical Comm. College
5293 High Point College
5348 John Wesley College
5333 Johnson C. Smith University
5351 Johnston Community College
5364 Lees-McRae College
5365 Lenoir-Rhyne College
5367 Livingstone College
5369 Louisburg College
5395 Mars Hill College
5410 Meredith College
5426 Methodist College
5423 Montreat-Anderson College
5435 Mount Olive College
5003 North Carolina A & T State Univ.
5495 North Carolina Central University
0388 North Carolina Loans-Health Science/Mathematics
5512 North Carolina Sch. of the Arts
5496 North Carolina St. Univ., Raleigh
5501 North Carolina Wesleyan College
5533 Peace College
5534 Pembroke State University
5536 Pfeiffer College
5301 Phillips Jr. Coll.—Hardbarger
5556 Pitt Community College
5544 Presbyterian Hospital Sch. of Nrsg.
5560 Queens College
5588 Richmond Community College
5594 Robeson Community College
5582 Rockingham Community College
5214 Saint Andrews Presbyterian Coll.
5596 Saint Augustine's College
5600 Saint Mary's College
5607 Salem College
5612 Shaw University
5651 Southeastern Community College
5667 Southwestern Community College
5644 Stanly Community College
5656 Surry Community College
5785 Tri-County Community College
University of North Carolina:
5013 —Asheville
5816 —Chapel Hill
5752 —Medicine
5105 —Charlotte
5913 —Greensboro
5907 —Wilmington
5885 Wake Forest University:
5084 —Bowman Gray Sch. of Med.
5937 —School of Law
5928 Wake Technical Comm. College
5886 Warren Wilson College
5926 Wayne Community College
5897 Western Carolina University
5921 Wilkes Community College
5908 Wingate College
5909 Winston-Salem State University

NORTH DAKOTA

0018 **North Dakota Student Financial Assistance Program**
6318 Jamestown College
6479 Minot State University
6474 North Dakota State University
6428 University of Mary
University of North Dakota:
6878 —Grand Forks
6905 —Williston

OHIO

Antioch University:
1017 —Antioch College
1652 —School for Adult and Experiential Learning
1002 Art Academy of Cincinnati
1021 Ashland University
1029 Athenaeum of Ohio
3203 Aultman Hospital Sch. of Nursing
1050 Baldwin-Wallace College
1072 Belmont Technical College
1067 Bluffton College
1069 Bowling Green State University, Bowling Green
8415 Bradford School
1099 Capital University:
1182 —Law & Grad. Center
Case Western Reserve University:
1105 —All Undergraduates
1112 —Applied Social Sciences
0694 —Dentistry
1092 —Graduate Studies
1110 —Law
0687 —Management
1104 —Medicine
3264 —Nursing-Graduate
1151 Cedarville College
1086 Central Ohio Technical College
1107 Central State University
1091 Cincinnati Bible College and Seminary
1984 Cincinnati Technical College
1088 Circleville Bible College
1127 Clark State Comm. College
1152 Cleveland Institute of Art
1124 Cleveland Institute of Music
1221 Cleveland State University
1129 College of Mount Saint Joseph
1134 College of Wooster
1085 Columbus Coll. of Art & Design
1148 Columbus State Community Coll.
8417 Community Hospital of Springfield
Cuyahoga Community College:
1978 —Eastern
1159 —Metropolitan
1985 —Western
1162 Defiance College
1164 Denison University
DeVry Institute of Technology:
1605 —Continuing Students
0344 —New Students
1178 Dyke College
1191 Edison State Community College
1219 Fairview Gen. Hosp. Sch. of Nrsg.
1133 Franciscan Univ. of Steubenville
1229 Franklin University
1259 Good Samaritan Hosp. Sch. of Nrsg.
1292 Heidelberg College
1297 Hiram College
1822 Hocking Technical College
1333 Jefferson Technical College
1342 John Carroll University
Kent State University:
1677 —Ashtabula
1814 —East Liverpool
1679 —Geauga
1367 —Kent
1684 —Salem
1678 —Stark
1381 —Trumbull
1682 —Tuscarawas
1370 Kenyon College
1386 Kettering College of Medical Arts
1391 Lake Erie College
1422 Lakeland Community College
1241 Lima Technical College
1417 Lorain County Community Coll.
1427 Lourdes College
1439 Malone College
9160 Mansfield Gen. Hosp. Sch. of Nrsg.
1444 Marietta College
9166 Mercy Hospital School of Nursing
1463 Miami Univ. (all campuses)
1502 Mount Carmel Sch./Coll. of Nrsg.
1492 Mount Union College
1531 Mount Vernon Nazarene College
1535 Muskingum Area Technical Coll.
1496 Muskingum College
1575 North Central Technical College
1235 Northwest Technical College
3260 Northwestern College
1566 Notre Dame College
1587 Oberlin College
4428 Ohio Diesel Technical Institute
1131 Ohio Dominican College
1591 Ohio Northern University
1592 Ohio State University
Ohio University:
1593 —Athens
9437 —Belmont
9494 —Chillicothe
0219 —Ironton
9682 —Lancaster
9761 —Portsmouth
9909 —Zanesville
1594 Ohio Wesleyan University
1597 Otterbein College
1643 Owens Technical College
9443 Providence Hosp. Sch. of Nrsg.
9555 RETS Technical Center
1695 Saint Elizabeth Hosp. Med. Center
1698 Saint Thomas Hosp. Medical Center
3241 Saint Vincent Medical Center
1790 Shawnee State University
1720 Sinclair Community College
1752 Southern State Comm. College
1688 Stark Technical College
1817 Tiffin University
1966 Union Institute
1829 University of Akron
1833 University of Cincinnati
1834 University of Dayton
1223 University of Findlay
1663 University of Rio Grande
1845 University of Toledo
1847 Urbana University
1848 Ursuline College
1926 Walsh College
1897 Washington State Comm. College
1906 Wilberforce University
1909 Wilmington College
1922 Wittenberg University
1179 Wright State University
1504 —School of Medicine
1965 Xavier University
1975 Youngstown State University

OKLAHOMA

6080 Cameron University
6117 Connors State College
6211 Flaming Rainbow University

5493 Newberry College
5494 North Amer. Inst. of Aviation
5498 North Greenville College
5550 Piedmont Tech. College
5540 Presbyterian College
9780 Sherman Coll. of Straight Chiropractic
0061 Sirrine Scholarship Program
5618 South Carolina State College
5627 Spartanburg Methodist College
5668 Spartanburg Technical College
5789 Tri-County Technical College
5049 Trident Technical College
University of South Carolina System:
5840 —Aiken
5845 —Beaufort
5837 —Coastal Caroline Coll., Conway
5818 —Columbia
5849 —Lancaster
5847 —Salkehatchie
5850 —Spartanburg
5821 —Sumter
5846 —Union
5863 Voorhees College
5910 Winthrop College
5912 Wofford College

SOUTH DAKOTA

0600 **South Dakota Student Incentive Grant Program**
6015 Augustana College
6042 Black Hills State University
6247 Dakota State University
6279 Huron University
6416 Mount Marty College
6652 So. Dakota Sch. of Mines & Tech.
6653 South Dakota State University
6881 Univ. of South Dakota, Vermillion

TENNESSEE

1028 Austin Peay State University
1058 Belmont University
1908 Bryan College
1102 Carson-Newman College
1121 Christian Brothers University
1161 David Lipscomb University
Draughon's Junior College:
9057 —Clarksville
4194 —Knoxville
3136 —Memphis
3261 —Nashville
1198 East Tennessee State University
1224 Fisk University
1230 Freed-Hardeman University
1298 Hiwassee College
1345 Johnson Bible College
1371 King College
1373 Knoxville College
1394 Lambuth College
1395 Lane College
1401 Lee College
1403 LeMoyne-Owen College
1408 Lincoln Memorial University
1454 Maryville College
1459 Memphis State University
1466 Middle Tennessee State Univ.
8859 Miller Motte Business College
1469 Milligan College
9318 Nashville Auto Diesel College
1648 Nashville State Tech. Institute
1795 Pellissippi State Tech. Comm College
1730 Rhodes College
4175 Rice College
1656 Roane State Comm. College
1725 Southern College of Optometry
1727 Southern College of SDA
1803 Tennessee State University
1804 Tennessee Technological Univ.
1805 Tennessee Wesleyan College
1809 Trevecca Nazarene College
1812 Tusculum College
1842 University of the South
University of Tennessee:
1831 —Chattanooga
1843 —Knoxville
1844 —Martin
1850 —Memphis, Center for Health Sciences
1871 Vanderbilt University:
1724 —Medical Center Allied Health
1883 —School of Medicine
1881 Volunteer State Community College
1893 Walters State Community College

TEXAS

6001 Abilene Christian University
6005 Alvin Community College
6570 Ambassador College
6644 Angelo State University
6209 Art Institute of Dallas
8271 Art Institute of Houston
6016 Austin College
6759 Austin Community College
6068 Bauder Fashion College
8639 Baumberger Endowment
6059 Baylor College of Dentistry
6052 Baylor College of Medicine
6032 Baylor University:
6032 —College of Nursing
6055 Bee County College
6043 Blinn College
6070 Brookhaven College
6148 Cedar Valley College
6133 College of the Mainland
6805 Collin County Comm. Coll. District
6849 Corpus Christi State University
6159 Dallas Baptist University
6160 Del Mar College
DeVry Institute of Technology:
6180 —Continuing Students
0372 —New/Transfer Students
6187 East Texas Baptist University
6188 East Texas St. Univ., Commerce
6201 Eastfield College
6199 El Centro College
6255 Galveston College
6254 Grayson County College
6268 Hardin-Simmons University
6282 Houston Baptist University
6296 Houston Community College
6280 Huston-Tillotson College
6303 Incarnate Word College
6319 Jarvis Christian College
6341 Kilgore College
Lamar University:
6360 —Beaumont
0441 —Orange
6589 —Port Arthur
6362 Laredo Junior College
6838 Laredo State University
6365 LeTourneau University
6369 Lon Morris College
6429 McLennan Community College
6402 McMurry University
6408 Midwestern State University
0401 Minnie Stevens Piper Fdtn.
6438 Mountain View College
6508 North Harris Montgomery CC Dist.
6519 North Lake College
6499 Northwood Institute
6550 Our Lady of the Lake University of San Antonio
9873 Parker College of Chiropractic
6577 Paul Quinn College
6580 Prairie View A & M University
6609 Rice University
6607 Richland College
6619 Saint Edward's University
6637 Saint Mary's University
6642 Saint Philip's College
6643 Sam Houston State University
6722 San Antonio Art Institute
6645 San Antonio College
San Jacinto College:
6694 —Central
6729 —North
6241 —South
6647 Schreiner College
6654 South Texas College of Law
6660 Southern Methodist University
6666 Southwest Texas Junior College
6667 Southwest Texas State Univ.
6671 Southwestern Adventist College
6705 Southwestern Christian College
6674 Southwestern University
6682 Stephen F. Austin State Univ.
6685 Sul Ross State University
6817 Tarleton State University
6834 Tarrant County Jr. Coll., Ft. Worth
6822 Texas A & I University
Texas A & M University:
6003 —College Station
6835 —Galveston
6820 Texas Christian University
6821 Texas College
6848 Texas College of Osteopathic Medicine
6823 Texas Lutheran College
6824 Texas Southern University:
6797 —Law School
6825 Texas Southmost College
6328 Texas State Tech. Inst., Waco
6827 Texas Tech University
6828 Texas Wesleyan University
6826 Texas Woman's University
6831 Trinity University
6833 Tyler Junior College
6868 University of Dallas
University of Houston:
6916 —Clear Lake City
6922 —Downtown College
6870 —University Park
6917 —Victoria
6481 University of North Texas
6880 University of Saint Thomas
University of Texas:
6013 —Arlington
6882 —Austin
6897 —Dallas
6829 —El Paso
6887 —Galveston Medical Branch
6888 —Houston Health Science Center
6919 —San Antonio
6908 —San Antonio Health Sci. Center
6686 —Southwestern Med. Center
6850 —Tyler
6915 Victoria College
6938 West Texas State University
6939 Wharton County Junior College
6940 Wiley College

UTAH

4019 Brigham Young University
4040 College of Eastern Utah
4283 Dixie College
4864 Salt Lake Comm. College
4727 Snow College
4092 Southern Utah University
4853 University of Utah
4857 Utah State University
4870 Utah Valley Comm. College
4941 Weber State University
4948 Westminster Coll. of Salt Lake City

VERMONT

3080 Bennington College
3944 Burlington College
3765 Castleton State College
3179 Center for Northern Studies
3291 Champlain College
3297 College of St. Joseph
3286 Community College of Vermont
3179 Fanny Allen Memorial School of Practical Nursing
3416 Goddard College
3418 Green Mountain College
3766 Johnson State College
3767 Lyndon State College
3509 Marlboro College
3526 Middlebury College:
3560 —Bread Loaf School of English
3179 New England Culinary Institute
3669 Norwich University:
3669 —The Russian School
3179 Putnam Memorial School of Practical Nursing
3757 Saint Michael's College
3788 School for International Training
3796 Southern Vermont College
3752 Sterling College
3179 Thompson Sch. for Practical Nrsg.
3900 Trinity College
3920 University of Vermont
3043 —Medical School
3669 Vermont College:
3669 —Adult Degree Program
3669 —Graduate Program
3669 —Master of Art Therapy
3669 —Master of Fine Arts in Writing
3179 Vermont College of Cosmetology
3941 Vermont Technical College

VIRGINIA

5017 Averett College
5083 Blue Ridge Community College
5063 Bluefield College
5069 Bridgewater College
5141 Central Virginia Comm. College
5691 Christendom College
5128 Christopher Newport College
5124 Clinch Valley College
5115 College of William and Mary in Virginia
5099 Community Hosp. of Roanoke Valley Coll. of Health Sciences
5163 Danville Community College
5181 Eastern Mennonite College
5844 Eastern Shore Community Coll.
5185 Emory and Henry College
5213 Ferrum College
5827 George Mason University
5276 Germanna Community College
5291 Hampden-Sydney College
5292 Hampton University
5294 Hollins College
5771 J. Sargent Reynolds Comm. Coll.
5392 James Madison University
5342 John Tyler Community College
Liberty University:
5385 —Main Campus
3499 —School of Lifelong Learning
5368 Longwood College
5381 Lord Fairfax Community College
5372 Lynchburg College
5397 Mary Baldwin College
5398 Mary Washington College
5405 Marymount University
1624 National College of Education
5513 New River Community College
5504 Norfolk Gen. Hosp. Sch. of Nrsg.
5864 Norfolk State University
Northern Virginia Community College:
5510 —Alexandria
5515 —Annandale
5774 —Manassas
5775 —Sterling
5517 —Woodbridge
5126 Old Dominion University
5549 Patrick Henry Community Coll.
5561 Piedmont Virginia Comm. Coll
5565 Radford University
5566 Randolph-Macon Coll., Ashland
5567 Randolph-Macon Woman's Coll., Lynchburg
Rappahannock Community College:
5590 —Glenns
5583 —Warsaw
5574 Richard Bland College
5580 Riverside Hosp. Sch. of Nrsg.
5571 Roanoke College
5604 Saint Paul's College
5613 Shenandoah University
5625 Southern Seminary College
5547 Southside Reg. Medical Center Sch. of Nursing
Southside Virginia Community College:
5660 —Christanna Campus
5669 —Keysville Campus
5659 Southwest Virginia Comm. Coll.
5634 Sweet Briar College
5793 Thomas Nelson Community Coll.
Tidewater Community College:
5707 —Chesapeake
5226 —Portsmouth
5787 —Virginia Beach
5569 University of Richmond
5820 University of Virginia:
3685 —School of Law
5753 —School of Medicine
5570 Virginia Commonwealth Univ.
5927 Virginia Highlands Comm. Coll.
5857 Virginia Intermont College
5858 Virginia Military Institute
5859 Virginia Polytech. Inst. & St. U.
5860 Virginia State University
5862 Virginia Union University
5867 Virginia Wesleyan College
5868 Virginia Western Comm. Coll.
5887 Washington and Lee University
5917 Wytheville Community College

WASHINGTON

7030 Antioch University
4805 Art Institute of Seattle
3170 Bastyr College
4029 Bellevue Community College
7077 Bellingham Technical School
4024 Big Bend Community College
4250 Bureau of Indian Affairs, Everett
4044 Central Washington University
4045 Centralia College
4042 City University
4055 Clark College
4147 Clover Park Voc. Tech. Institute
4077 Columbia Basin College
4801 Cornish College of the Arts
8556 Divers Institute of Technology
4301 Eastern Washington University
4307 Edmonds Community College
4303 Everett Community College
4292 Evergreen State College
4330 Gonzaga University
4332 Grays Harbor College
4337 Green River Community College
4344 Heritage College
4348 Highline Community College
9022 L.H. Bates Voc. Tech. Institute
9023 Lake Washington Voc. Tech. Inst.
4402 Lower Columbia College
4408 Lutheran Bible Institute of Seattle
4554 North Seattle Community College
4541 Northwest College of the Assemblies of God
4583 Olympic College
4597 Pacific Lutheran University
4615 Peninsula College
4369 Perry Technical Institute
4103 Pierce College
4618 Puget Sound Christian College
7749 Renton Voc. Tech. Institute
4674 Saint Martin's College
4741 Seattle Central Community Coll.
4694 Seattle Pacific University
4695 Seattle University
4738 Shoreline Community College
4699 Skagit Valley College
4578 South Puget Sound Comm. Coll.
4759 South Seattle Community College
4739 Spokane Community College
4752 Spokane Falls Community Coll.
4826 Tacoma Community College
7849 Trend College
4067 University of Puget Sound:
7360 —School of Law
4854 Univ. of Washington, Seattle
4940 Walla Walla Coll., College Place
4963 Walla Walla Community College
4705 Washington State University
4942 Wenatchee Valley College
4947 Western Washington University
4974 Whatcom Community College
4951 Whitman College
4953 Whitworth College
4993 Yakima Valley Comm. College

WEST VIRGINIA

5005 Alderson-Broaddus College
5034 Appalachian Bible College
5054 Beckley College
5060 Bethany College
5064 Bluefield State College
5120 Concord College
5151 Davis and Elkins College
5211 Fairmont State College
5254 Glenville State College
5268 Greenbrier Community Coll. Ctr.
5396 Marshall University
5519 Ohio Valley College
5539 Potomac State College
5635 Saint Mary's Hosp. Sch. of Nrsg.
5608 Salem-Teikyo University
5615 Shepherd College
Southern West Virginia Comm. College:
5446 —Logan
5447 —Williamson
5419 University of Charleston
5946 Webster College
5901 West Liberty State College
5902 West Virginia Inst. of Tech.
5942 West Virginia Northern Community College
5903 West Virginia State College
5932 West Virginia Univ. at Parkersburg
West Virginia University:
5904 —Main Campus
5949 —Health Science Center
5905 West Virginia Wesleyan College
5906 Wheeling Jesuit College

WISCONSIN

1012 Alverno College
1046 Bellin College of Nursing
1059 Beloit College
1043 Blackhawk Technical College
1100 Cardinal Stritch College
1101 Carroll College
1103 Carthage College
1139 Concordia University
1202 Edgewood College
1217 Fox Valley Technical College
Gateway Technical College:
1243 —Kenosha
1255 —Racine
3619 LaCrosse School of Beauty Culture
1393 Lakeland College
1398 Lawrence University
1536 Madison Area Tech. College
1443 Marian College of Fond du Lac
1448 Marquette University
1519 Medical College of Wisconsin
1475 Milwaukee Area Technical Coll.
3220 Milwaukee Coll. of Business
7590 Milwaukee Inst. of Art & Design
1476 Milwaukee Sch. of Engineering
Moraine Park Technical College:
1433 —Beaver Dam
1499 —Fond du Lac
4174 —West Bend
1490 Mount Mary College
1512 Mount Senario College
4190 Northeast Wisconsin Tech. College
1561 Northland College
1563 Northwestern College
1664 Ripon College
1706 Saint Norbert College
1300 Silver Lake College
1694 Southwest Wisconsin Tech. Coll.
University of Wisconsin:
1913 —Eau Claire
1859 —Green Bay
1914 —La Crosse
1846 —Madison
1473 —Milwaukee
1916 —Oshkosh
1860 —Parkside/Kenosha
1917 —Platteville
1918 —River Falls
1919 —Stevens Point
1740 —Stout
1920 —Superior
1921 —Whitewater
1999 University of Wisconsin Centers (All Two-Year Campuses)
1878 Viterbo College
1087 Western Wisconsin Tech. College
3618 Wisconsin College of Cosmetology
1513 Wisconsin Lutheran College
1903 Wisconsin School of Electronics

WYOMING

4043 Casper College
4115 Central Wyoming College
4700 Eastern Wyoming College
4415 Laramie County Comm. College
4542 Northwest Community College
4536 Sheridan College
4855 University of Wyoming
4957 Western Wyoming College
4977 Wyoming Technical Institute

SUZANNE S. STUDENT

Social Security Number:________________

Home Address:____

____

Home Phone: ____________________

Birthdate:______________________

High School: Anytown High School
Anytown, U.S.A.

Guidance Counselor:____

Graduation Date: June 1993

G.P.A.: 3.24 Ranking: Upper One-Third SAT Scores: Taken 11/92

Probable Area of Academic Concentration: Finance with Music minor

---

Activities, Awards & Honors
Recipient of Ethel Smith Award for Musicianship and Character

Marching Band: Senior Drum Major, Conductor of 120-piece band (Note: School placed First in County competition and Second in State competition)

Suzanne S. Student was awarded First Place as Best Drum Major in County competition.

Publications: Yearbook Business Manager

Student Government: Senior class representative

Athletics: Official Scorekeeper, Boy's Varsity Basketball Team

---

Work Experience: Assistant to Bookkeeper, Anytown Hospital
Cashier, A&P Supermarkets

Personal Statement

A special interest I have is in traveling. So far in my seventeen years, I have been able to travel a significant amount of time. I have been in Hong Kong, Thailand, Amsterdam, Germany and even East Berlin before the wall came tumbling down.

Three years ago, I was selected to go on a special student exchange to Germany. I lived with a family in Buxtehude, West Germany. While staying with them, I was able to experience their culture; it was a valuable learning experience.

While with them, I visited the Bergen-Belsen Concentration Camp, the one in which Anne Frank died. It certainly made me more aware of what could happen if my generation doesn't pull together and help make this a better world.

Also, I was invited into East Germany by the East German Government and was able to see, at first-hand, the difference between that form of government, and what it means to the people, and our own. In retrospect, it is quite apparent why there is now no wall.

STUART S. STUDENT

Address:
Phone Number:
Social Security Number:
Birthdate:

Academic
High School:
Guidance Counselor:
Grade Point Average:
Class Curriculum:
SAT Score:
Date of Graduation:
College Course Desired:

Personal
Height:
Weight:
Handedness: Left
Time: 5.0 seconds at 40 yards with equipment on

Athletics
Football:
1992: Varsity/Starting Quarterback, Starting Outside Linebacker
1991: Varsity/Starting Outside Linebacker/Backup Quarterback
1990: Junior Varsity/Starting Quarterback/Starting Outside Linebacker

Honors: All-League Selection, Captain
Coach: Phone:

Final Statistics - 1992 Season

Offense: Quarterback/Number 13/Maroon Jersey in tapes

Passing
Att 132/Comp 59/Pct 45%/Ydg 750/Avg per catch 12.71/LP 60/TDs 14
Rushing
Att 59/Ydg 276/Avg 4.7/Longest 35/Touchdowns 3
Receiving
Number 3/Ydg 49/Avg 16.3/Longest 23
Punts
Number 3/Ydg 103/Avg 34.3/Longest 59
Field Goals
Att 1/Comp 1
Defense: Outside Linebacker
Sacks 3/First Hits 11/Second Hits 4

Wrestling:

Weight Class: 167

Record
(exclusive of senior year)

Junior: Won 11 Lost 3 (League Qualifying Champion)
Sophomore: Won 9 Lost 3 (League Qualifying Champion)
Freshman: Won 9 Lost 0 (League Qualifying Champion)

Tournaments: First, County Take-Down
Second, State Finals
First, Junior Mets
Second, League Championships

Coach: Phone:

Extra-Curricular Activities

Senior Class Vice President
All-County Band

Special Honors

Herb Jones Award as Outstanding Student-Athlete

Hobbies

Boat building. Built own clamboat.

Stuart S. Student
100 Main Street
Anytown, U.S.A. 00000

PERSONAL STATEMENT

In 1990, I started work on a project that took me two and a half years to complete. This was the building of my own 25-foot clam boat.

The beginning point was when my father came home one morning with an old cutdown empty boat hull. Since I enjoyed fishing, I was told that this would aid me. At first, I was a little surprised. Did my father expect me to build my own boat? He did, but soon that initial doubt was replaced with a combination of ambition mixed with anxiety.

I started the design that very day, laying out the plans on graph paper. I also listed what materials were needed to construct the boat. The physical work, with some general guidance from my father, would begin the next day.

The first thing that had to be accomplished was the cleaning-out of the hull. In effect, I was starting from scratch, building this boat from the ground up. Within three months, I had the supports for the floor in and was ready to assemble the actual flooring. This constituted step one of the construction process.

After building the floor, I began to raise the sides of the hull so that I'd have a little walkway around the boat. Following this, it was time to lay out the deck and fasten it. Another three months. Then, the cabin was ready to be built; that would take the longest period of time. After all, I had school, football, wrestling, band practice and a few odd jobs to do when I was not working on the boat. So, what started out in terms of months, became years.

It was now 1992 and the goal that I set two years before was on the road to accomplishment. Excitement grew as the boat neared completion.

The 1992 winter passed and within a few months, the boat was being painted...the last process. Finally, it was ready for the big test. Would it float?

On June 1, 1992, we found out. As my boat was lowered into the bay, I had the most extraordinary feeling of my life: it was an accomplishment second to none.

I learned many things about myself during two and a half years, the most important ones being discipline and my ability to do something if I really wanted it badly enough. I also learned to have confidence in myself and to realize that no matter how frustrating little failures may be (and there were plenty along the way), patience and tenacity still make the final product worth all the trouble.

Other important things that I experienced were the budgeting of money and the need for careful planning. Throughout the entire process of building this boat, I had to decide what materials to buy and how I could get the best quality for the least amount of money., Certainly for a 15-year old, the problem of budgeting money properly was an achievement in itself.

There are many clammers on the bay, but I have joined the special group of boat builders who have the knowledge that they truly "own" their boats as well as pilot them.

FAF® Financial Aid Form — School Year 1992-93

Warning: If you purposely give false or misleading information, you may be subject to a $10,000 fine, a prison sentence, or both.

Do not write in this space

NY 43

Use only a No. 2 (soft-lead) pencil. Don't write outside of the boxes or answer spaces. "You" and "your" on this form always mean the student who wants aid.

Section A — Student's Identification Information

1. Your name ☐ Last ☐ First ☐ M.I.

2. Your permanent mailing address (Mail will be sent to this address. See page 2 for state/country abbreviation.)
Number, street, and apartment number
City State Zip Code

3. Your title (optional) 1 ☐ Mr. 2 ☐ Miss, Ms., or Mrs.

4. Your state of legal residence ☐

5. Your social security number ☐ - ☐ - ☐

6. Your date of birth Month Day Year

7. Are you a U.S. citizen? (Mark only one box.)
1 ☐ Yes, I am a U.S. citizen.
2 ☐ No, but I am an eligible noncitizen. (See the instructions on page 2.)
A ☐
3 ☐ No, neither of the above. (See the instructions on page 2.)

8. As of today, are you married? (Mark only one box.)
1 ☐ I am not married. (I am single, divorced, or widowed.)
2 ☐ I am married.
3 ☐ I am separated from my spouse.

9. What year will you be in college in 1992-93? (Mark only one box.)
1 ☐ 1st (never previously attended college)
2 ☐ 1st (previously attended college)
3 ☐ 2nd
4 ☐ 3rd
5 ☐ 4th
6 ☐ 5th or more undergraduate
7 ☐ first year graduate/professional (beyond a bachelor's degree)
8 ☐ continuing graduate or professional

10. Will you have your first bachelor's degree before July 1, 1992? Yes ☐ 1 No ☐ 2

Section B — Student Status

11. a. Were you born **before** January 1, 1969? Yes ☐ 1 No ☐ 2
b. Are you a veteran of the U.S. Armed Forces? Yes ☐ 1 No ☐ 2
c. Are you a ward of the court or are both your parents dead? Yes ☐ 1 No ☐ 2
d. Do you have legal dependents (other than a spouse) that fit the definition on page 3 of the instructions? Yes ☐ 1 No ☐ 2

- If you answered "Yes" to any part of question **11**, go to Section C and fill in the **GRAY and the WHITE areas** on the rest of the form. Some colleges may also ask you to complete the **PURPLE** areas. (Skip questions **12** through **15**.)
- If you answered "No" to every part of question **11** and you are:
  — unmarried now (single, divorced, separated, or widowed) **and** will be an undergraduate student in 1992-93, answer question **12**. (Skip question **15**.)
  — married now or will be a graduate/professional student in 1992-93, answer question **15**. (Skip questions **12** through **14f**.)

Unmarried Undergraduate Students Only

12. Did your parents claim you as an income tax exemption ... in 1990? Yes ☐ 1 No ☐ 2 ... in 1991? Yes ☐ 1 No ☐ 2

- If you answered "Yes" to **either** year in question **12**, go to Section C and fill in the **areas outlined in PURPLE and the WHITE areas** on the rest of the form. (Skip questions **13** through **15**.)
- If you answered "No" to **both** years in question **12**, answer question **13** below.

13. Beginning with the 1987-88 school year, when did you **first** receive federal student financial aid? (Mark only one box. See instructions on page 3.)

13		14		Yes	No		Yes	No
1 ☐ In the 1987-88 school year (Answer **14a** only.)	→	**14. a.** Did you have total resources of $4,000 or more, not including parents' support	... in 1985?	☐ 1	☐ 2	... in 1986?	☐ 1	☐ 2
2 ☐ In the 1988-89 school year (Answer **14b** only.)	→	**14. b.** Did you have total resources of $4,000 or more, not including parents' support	... in 1986?	☐ 1	☐ 2	... in 1987?	☐ 1	☐ 2
3 ☐ In the 1989-90 school year (Answer **14c** only.)	→	**14. c.** Did you have total resources of $4,000 or more, not including parents' support	... in 1987?	☐ 1	☐ 2	... in 1988?	☐ 1	☐ 2
4 ☐ In the 1990-91 school year (Answer **14d** only.)	→	**14. d.** Did you have total resources of $4,000 or more, not including parents' support	... in 1988?	☐ 1	☐ 2	... in 1989?	☐ 1	☐ 2
5 ☐ In the 1991-92 school year (Answer **14e** only.)	→	**14. e.** Did you have total resources of $4,000 or more, not including parents' support	... in 1989?	☐ 1	☐ 2	... in 1990?	☐ 1	☐ 2
6 ☐ In none of the above. (Answer **14f** only.)	→	**14. f.** Did you have total resources of $4,000 or more, not including parents' support	... in 1990?	☐ 1	☐ 2	... in 1991?	☐ 1	☐ 2

- If you answered "No" to **either** year in question **14a, 14b, 14c, 14d, 14e,** or **14f**, fill in the **areas outlined in PURPLE and the WHITE areas** on the rest of the form. Go to Section C.
- If you answered "Yes" to **both** years in question **14a, 14b, 14c, 14d, 14e,** or **14f**, fill in the **areas outlined in GRAY and the WHITE areas** on the rest of the form. Some colleges may also ask you to complete the **PURPLE** areas. Go to Section C.

Married Students or Graduate/Professional Students Only

15. Will your parents claim you as an income tax exemption in 1992? Yes ☐ 1 No ☐ 2

- If you answered "Yes" to question **15**, fill in the **areas outlined in PURPLE and the WHITE areas** on the rest of the form. Go to Section C.
- If you answered "No" to question **15**, fill in the **areas outlined in GRAY and the WHITE areas** on the rest of the form. Some colleges may also ask you to complete the **PURPLE** areas. Go to Section C.

Section C — Household Information

Parents

16. What is your parents' current marital status? (Mark only one box.)
1 ☐ single 2 ☐ married 3 ☐ separated 4 ☐ divorced 5 ☐ widowed

17. What is your parents' state of legal residence? ☐

18. Number of family members in 1992-93
Always include yourself (the student) and your parents. Include your parents' other children and other people only if they meet the definition on page 3 of the instructions. ☐

19. Number of college students in 1992-93
Of the number in 18, write in the number of family members who will be in college at least half-time. Include yourself — the student who is applying for aid. ☐

Student (and Spouse)

20. Number of family members in 1992-93
Always include yourself and your spouse. Include your children and other people only if they meet the definition on page 3 of the instructions. ☐

21. Number of college students in 1992-93
Of the number in **20**, write in the number of family members who will be in college at least half-time. Include yourself. ☐

Copyright © 1991 by College Entrance Examination Board. All rights reserved.

Print your name Last First

Section D — 1991 Income, Earnings, and Benefits (You must see the instructions for income and taxes that you should exclude from questions 24 through 28.)

Everyone must fill out the Student (and Spouse) column below.

Student (and Spouse)

22. The following 1991 U.S. income tax return figures are (Mark only one box.)
- 1 from a completed 1991 IRS Form 1040EZ or 1040A. (Go to **23.**)
- 2 from a completed 1991 IRS Form 1040. (Go to **23.**)
- 3 estimated. Will file 1991 IRS Form 1040EZ or 1040A. (Go to **23.**)
- 4 estimated. Will file 1991 IRS Form 1040. (Go to **23.**)
- 5 a tax return will not be filed. (Skip to **26.**)

Tax Filers Only

23. 1991 total number of exemptions (IRS Form 1040 — line 6e, 1040A — line 6e, or 1040EZ — see instructions on page 4)

24. 1991 Adjusted Gross Income (AGI) — IRS Form 1040 — line 31, 1040A — line 16, or 1040EZ — line 3. (See instructions on page 4.) — 24. $ .00 | 24. $ .00

25. 1991 U.S. income tax paid (IRS Form 1040 — line 46, 1040A — line 25, or 1040EZ — line 7) — 25. $ .00 | 25. $ .00

26. 1991 income earned from work by **Father** 26. $ .00 | **Student** 26. $ .00

27. 1991 income earned from work by **Mother** 27. $ .00 | **Spouse** 27. $ .00

28. 1991 untaxed income and benefits (yearly totals only)
- **a.** 1991 Social security benefits — 28a. $ .00 | 28a. $ .00
- **b.** 1991 Aid to Families with Dependent Children (AFDC or ADC) — b. $ .00 | b. $ .00
- **c.** 1991 Child support received for all children — c. $ .00 | c. $ .00
- **d.** Other untaxed 1991 income and benefits from Worksheet II on page 8 of the instructions — d. $ .00 | d. $ .00

Section E — Stafford Loan Information (Formerly Guaranteed Student Loan [GSL])

If you have never received a Stafford Loan (GSL) or a Federal Insured Student Loan (FISL), go to question **34**. Skip questions **29** through **33**.

29. What is the total unpaid principal balance on all your Stafford Loans (GSLs)? (If you answered "0," go to question **34**. Skip questions **30-33**.) $ .00

30. What is the total unpaid principal balance on your **most recent** Stafford Loan (GSL)? $ .00

31. What is the interest rate of your **most recent** Stafford Loan (GSL)? 1 ☐ 7% 2 ☐ 8% 3 ☐ 9% 4 ☐ 8/10%

32. What was the loan period of your **most recent** Stafford Loan (GSL)? from Month Year through Month Year

33. What was your class level when you received your **most recent** Stafford Loan (GSL)?
- 1 ☐ Freshman
- 2 ☐ Sophomore
- 3 ☐ Junior
- 4 ☐ Senior
- 5 ☐ 5th-year or more undergraduate
- 6 ☐ 1st-year graduate/professional (beyond a bachelor's degree)
- 7 ☐ Continuing graduate or professional

Section F — Federal Student Aid Releases and Certification

34. What college(s) do you plan to go to in 1992-93?

	Name	City and State	CSS Code No.
a.			
b.			
c.			

35. Do you give the U.S. Department of Education permission to send information from this form to:
- — the financial aid agencies in your state? Yes ☐ 1 No ☐ 2
- — the college(s) you named in **34** (or its representative)? Yes ☐ 1 No ☐ 2

Note: By marking "Yes" you are not applying for state and institutional aid in some states. Some agencies and colleges that use the FAF also require that a CSS report be sent to them. See instructions.

36. Are you in default on a federal student loan, or do you owe a refund on a federal student grant? (Mark only one box.)
- 1 ☐ I am in default on a federal student loan.
- 2 ☐ I owe a refund on a federal student grant.
- 3 ☐ Both of the above
- 4 ☐ None of the above

37. Mark this box if you give Selective Service permission to register you. (See instructions.) ☐

38. **Certification:** All of the information on this form and the Supplemental Information, if completed, is true and complete to the best of my knowledge. I realize that information from this form will be sent to the U.S. Department of Education for the purpose of determining federal student aid eligibility. If asked by an authorized official, I agree to give proof of the information that I have given on this form and the Supplemental Information, if completed. I realize that this proof may include a copy of my U.S., state, or local income tax return. I also realize that if I don't give proof when asked, the student may be denied aid.

Everyone giving information on this form must sign below. If you don't sign the form, it will be returned unprocessed.

1 Student's signature

2 Student's spouse's signature

3 Father's (Stepfather's) signature

4 Mother's (Stepmother's) signature

Date this form was completed:
Write in the month and day. Month Day
Mark the year. 1 ☐ 1992 2 ☐ 1993 Year

IMPORTANT: You must read page 5 of the instructions to see if you need to fill out Sections G through J.

SUPPLEMENTAL INFORMATION

Section G — 1991 Expenses

39. 1991 medical and dental expenses not paid by insurance — 39. $ .00 | 39. $ .00

40. 1991 elementary, junior high, and high school tuition for dependent children
- **a.** Amount paid (Don't include tuition paid for the applicant.) — 40a. $ .00 | 40a. $ .00
- **b.** For how many dependent children? (Don't include the applicant.) — b. | b.

Section H — Asset Information

If you are completing this section, you must fill out the Student (and Spouse) columns below.

Parents

41. Is either of your parents a displaced homemaker? (See instructions on page 6.) — 41. Yes ☐ 1 No ☐ 2
42. Write in the age of your older parent. — 42. ____

		What is it worth today?	What is owed on it?
43.	Cash, savings, and checking accounts	$ .00	XXXXXXXXXXXXX
44.	Home (Renters write in "0.")	$ .00	$ .00
45.	Other real estate and investments	$ .00	$ .00
46.	Business and farm	$ .00	$ .00

47. Does any part of **46** include a farm? — 47. Yes ☐ 1 No ☐ 2

Student (and Spouse)

41. Are you, or is your spouse, a displaced homemaker? (See instructions.) Yes ☐ 1 No ☐ 2
42. XXXXXXXXXXXXX

	What is it worth today?	What is owed on it?
43.	$ .00	XXXXXXXXXXXXX
44.	$ .00	$ .00
45.	$ .00	$ .00
46.	$ .00	$ .00

47. Yes ☐ 1 No ☐ 2

Section I — Student's Monthly Veterans Educational Benefits

(Expected Amount July 1, 1992 — June 30, 1993) (If you are completing this section, you must answer question **48**. If you are filling out the gray and white areas, you must also answer question **49**.)

48. Your veterans Dependents Educational Assistance Program Benefits
   - **a.** Amount per month $ ____ .00
   - **b.** Number of months ☐☐

49. Your VEAP Benefits
   - **a.** Amount per month $ ____ .00
   - **b.** Number of months ☐☐

Section J — Expected 1992 Taxable & Nontaxable Income & Benefits

(You must see the instructions for income and taxes that you should exclude from questions **51** through **55**.)

If you are completing this section, you must fill out the Student (and Spouse) column below.

Parents

50. Is either parent **certified** as a dislocated worker by the appropriate agency? (See instructions on page 6.) — 50. Yes ☐ 1 No ☐ 2

			Parents
51.	1992 income earned from work by	**Father**	$ .00
52.	1992 income earned from work by	**Mother**	$ .00
53.	1992 other taxable income		$ .00
54.	1992 U.S. income tax to be paid		$ .00
55.	1992 nontaxable income and benefits (See instructions on page 6.)		$ .00

Student (and Spouse)

Are you, or is your spouse, **certified** as a dislocated worker by the appropriate agency? (See instructions on page 7.) — 50. Yes ☐ 1 No ☐ 2

		Student (and Spouse)
Student	51.	$ .00
Spouse	52.	$ .00
	53.	$ .00
	54.	$ .00
	55.	$ .00

Section K — Student's Other Information

56. Your home telephone ☐☐☐ – ☐☐☐ – ☐☐☐☐ (Area Code, Number)
57. Date you began living in your state of legal residence Month ☐☐ Year ☐☐
58. If you have dependents other than a spouse, **how many** will be in each of the following age groups during 1992-93? Ages 0-5 ☐ Ages 6-12 ☐ Ages 13+ ☐
59. If you are now in high school, give your high school 6-digit code number. ☐☐☐☐☐☐
60. **a.** List all colleges that you have attended. Begin with college you attended most recently.

Name, city, and state of college	Period of attendance From (mo./yr.)	To (mo./yr.)	CSS Code Number

   b. If you have previously attended more than three colleges, write in the total number of colleges you have attended. ☐

61. Your course of study code (See instructions.) ☐☐

62. Date you expect to complete your current college degree/certificate Month ☐☐ Year ☐☐
63. Your expected enrollment status during the 1992-93 school year (Mark only one box.)
   1 ☐ Full-time 2 ☐ Three-quarter time 3 ☐ Half-time 4 ☐ Less than half-time
64. During the 1992-93 school year, you want financial aid from ☐☐ Month ☐☐ Year through ☐☐ Month ☐☐ Year
65. Mark your preference for work or loan assistance.
   1 ☐ Part-time job only
   2 ☐ Part-time job and loan (including Stafford Loan)
   3 ☐ Loan only (including Stafford Loan)
   4 ☐ No preference (including Stafford Loan)

   Mark only one box. If you mark box 2, 3, or 4, your FAF information will be sent to the New York State Higher Education Services Corporation (NYSHESC).
66. **a.** Your occupation/employer ____
   b. Employer's address ____
   c. Will you continue to work for this employer during the 1992-93 school year? Yes ☐ 1 No ☐ 2
67. **a.** Your driver's license number ☐☐☐☐☐☐☐☐☐☐☐☐☐☐☐☐☐☐☐☐
   b. State that issued the above driver's license number State ☐☐

Section L — Student's Expected Summer/School-Year Income

(See instructions for the kinds of income to exclude.)

		Summer 1992 3 months	School Year 1992-93 9 months
68.	Income earned from work by you	$ .00	$ .00
69.	Income earned from work by your spouse	$ .00	$ .00
70.	Other taxable income	$ .00	$ .00
71.	Nontaxable income and benefits	$ .00	$ .00

Section M — Student's Expected Other Veterans Benefits

(July 1, 1992 – June 30, 1993)

72. Other benefits administered by the Veterans Administration (See page 7 of instructions. Don't include any benefits you already reported in **48** or **49**.)
   - **a.** Amount per month $
   - **b.** Number of months ☐☐

73. **a.** Year of separation ☐☐ Year of divorce ☐☐
   b. Other parent's name ____
   Home address ____
   Occupation/Employer ____
   c. According to court order, when will support for the student end? Month ☐☐ Year ☐☐
   d. Who claimed the student as a tax exemption for 1991? ____
   e. Is there an agreement specifying a contribution for the student's education? Yes ☐ No ☐
   If yes, how much for the 1992-93 school year? $ ____ .00

Section O — Family Members' Listing

Give information for all family members included in **18** or **20** but don't give information about yourself. List up to seven other family members here. If more than seven, list first those who will be in college at least half-time.

74.

	Full name of family member	Age	Relationship (Use code below.)	In the 1992-93 school year, will attend college for at least one term: full-time	half-time	Name of school or college this person will attend in 1992-93 school year	Year in school 1992-93	Occupation/Employer of this person	If attended college in 1991-92, give amount of: 1991-92 Scholarships/Grants	1991-92 Parents' Contribution
1	You — the Student Applicant									
2			☐	1 ☐	2 ☐					
3			☐	1 ☐	2 ☐					
4			☐	1 ☐	2 ☐					
5			☐	1 ☐	2 ☐					
6			☐	1 ☐	2 ☐					
7			☐	1 ☐	2 ☐					
8			☐	1 ☐	2 ☐					

Write in the correct code from the right.
1 = Student's parent 2 = Student's stepparent 3 = Student's brother or sister 4 = Student's husband or wife 5 = Student's son or daughter 6 = Student's grandparent 7 = Other

[illegible]

$ .00

a. year purchased 1 9

b. purchase price $ .00

$ .00

a. $ .00

b. $ .00

c. $ .00

d. $ .00

e. $ .00

f. $ .00

g. $ .00

Section Q — Student's Colleges & Programs

79. List the names and CSS code numbers of up to eight colleges and programs to which you want CSS to send information from this form. Give the correct housing code. Don't list NYSHESC or federal student aid programs. Be sure to include the college(s) you listed in **34**. Enclose the right fee. See the instructions and **80**.

Name	City and State	CSS Code No.	Housing Code*

***Housing Codes for 1992-93** (Enter only one code for each college.)
1 = With parents 2 = Campus housing 3 = Off-campus housing 4 = With relatives

80. Fee: Mark the box that tells how many colleges and programs are listed in **79**.

CSS Only

1 ☐ **$9.75** 3 ☐ **$25.25** 5 ☐ **$40.75** 7 ☐ **$56.25**
2 ☐ **$17.50** 4 ☐ **$33.00** 6 ☐ **$48.50** 8 ☐ **$64.00**

CSS Use Only

Mail this form with a check or money order for the right amount made out to CSS.

81. For the first college in New York State that you listed in **79**, mark all the terms for which you are requesting payment during the 1992-93 school year.
1 ☐ Summer 1992 2 ☐ Fall 1992 3 ☐ Winter 1992-93 4 ☐ Spring 1993

82. For the first college in New York State that you listed in **79**, mark this box if you are requesting payment for only a New York State Scholarship or other non-need-based award. (See page NY-2 of the instructions.) ☐

83. For the first college in New York State that you listed in **79**, will you be enrolled in a HEOP, EOP, SEEK, CD, or five-year bachelor's degree program? Yes ☐ 1 No ☐ 2

Section R — Explanations/Special Circumstances

If there are special circumstances that will affect your eligibility, write to the colleges to which you are applying.

CSS Use Only 5 6

Section S — New York State Tuition Assistance Program (TAP) and Scholarship Questions

43

84. If you listed a college in New York State in **79**, do you give CSS permission to send information from this FAF to the New York State Higher Education Services Corporation (NYSHESC) as application for the Tuition Assistance Program (TAP)? By marking "Yes" you also authorize the NYS Department of Taxation and Finance to release to NYSHESC certified copies of your personal tax returns for all periods reported in Section S. Yes ☐ 1 No ☐ 2

85. If you are claiming that you are financially independent of your parents for purposes of New York State financial aid programs, read page NY-2 of the instructions. Complete the worksheet provided and mark the appropriate box. 1 ☐ 2 ☐

86. Reporting Incomes: Earlier sections of this form asked you to report total federal income. New York State Tuition Assistance Program (TAP) awards are based on New York State net taxable income or the equivalent. Carefully read the instructions for **86a-b** on page NY-3 before entering the incomes and number of exemptions.

a. Student's NYS net taxable income (Include spouse's income and exemptions if you are married.) $ .00 Number of exemptions

b. Parents' NYS net taxable income (Read the instructions on page NY-3 carefully.) $ .00 Number of exemptions

87. a. Father's last name (first 3 letters) b. Social Security no. - -

c. Mother's last name (first 3 letters) d. Social Security no. - -

88. Parent's NYS Income Exclusion: Read page NY-3 of the instructions before answering this question. Only one parent's income can be excluded for separation/divorce.

a. To exclude FATHER'S income if: 1 ☐ FATHER died 2 ☐ separated or divorced — Give earliest date: Month Year

b. To exclude MOTHER'S income if: 1 ☐ MOTHER died 2 ☐ separated or divorced — Give earliest date: Month Year

c. Write in the amount of support received for you during 1991 from the parent whose income is to be excluded. **(If none, write in "0.")** $ .00

89. Write in the amount of other 1992-93 expected educational aid from the worksheet on page NY-4 of the instructions. $ .00

90. If you (the student) are married, write in spouse's social security number here and enter date of marriage in **91** below. - -

91. If you (the student) are separated/divorced or widowed, enter earliest date on which you were separated/divorced or widowed, rather than date of marriage. Month Year

92. a. Are you or will you be a graduate of a New York State high school or a recipient of a GED in New York State? Yes ☐ 1 No ☐ 2

b. Date of graduation or receipt of GED Month Year

EVALUATION CHART

NAME ______________________________

ADDRESS ______________________________

____

PHONE NUMBER ______________________________

DIRECTOR OF ADMISSIONS ______________________________

FOUNDED ______________________________

AFFILIATION ______________________________

LOCATION ______________________________

CAMPUS ______________________________

FACULTY ______________________________

ENROLLMENT ______________________________

LAST FRESHMAN CLASS ______________________________

____

STUDENTS ______________________________

____

____

COSTS ______________________________

FINANCIAL AID ______________________________

RATING ______________________________

BIBLIOGRAPHY

Barron's Profiles of American Colleges. New York: Barron's Educational Series, 1992.

Bernbach, *Lisa. College Book.* New York: Ballantine, 1990.

Cass, James & Birnbaum, Max. *Comparative Guide to American Colleges.* New York: HarperCollins, 1990.

Fiske, Edward B. *The Fiske Guide to Colleges.* New York: Times Books, 1992.

How to Afford the College of Your Choice. Albany, New York: Commission on Independent Colleges and Universities, 1992.

Lovejoy's College Guide. New York: Prentice Hall, 1991.

NCAA Guide for the College-Bound Student-Athlete. Overland Park, Kansas: The National Collegiate Athletic Association, 1992.

Peterson's Four-Year Colleges. Princeton: Peterson's Guides, 1992.

The College Handbook. New York: College Entrance Examination Board, 1992.

Yale Daily News. *The Insiders Guide to the Colleges.* New York: St. Martin's Press, 1991.

BIBLIOGRAPHY

Barron's Profiles of American Colleges. New York: Barron's Educational Series, 1992.

Birnbach, Lisa. *College Book.* New York: Ballantine, [illegible]

Cass, James & Birnbaum, Max. *Comparative Guide to American Colleges.* New York: HarperCollins, [illegible]

Fiske, Edward B. *The Fiske Guide to Colleges.* New York: Times Books, 1992.

[illegible] College [illegible]. Albany, New York: Commission on Independent Colleges and Universities, 1992.

[illegible] Guide. New York: [illegible], [illegible]

NCAA Guide for the College-Bound Student-Athlete. Overland Park, Kansas: The National Collegiate Athletic Association, [illegible]

Peterson's Four-Year Colleges. Princeton: Peterson's Guides, [illegible]

The College Handbook. New York: College Entrance Examination Board, [illegible]

Yale Daily News. *The Insider's Guide to the Colleges.* New York: St. Martin's Press, [illegible]

INDEX

ALLWORTH BOOKS

Allworth Press publishes quality books to help individuals and small businesses. Titles include:

Legal-Wise: Self-Help Legal Forms for Everyone *by Carl Battle* (208 pages, 8½" X 11", $16.95)

Business and Legal Forms for Authors and Self-Publishers *by Tad Crawford* (176 pages, 8⅞" X 11", $15.95)

Business and Legal Forms for Fine Artists *by Tad Crawford* (128 pages, 8⅞" X 11", $12.95)

Business and Legal Forms for Graphic Designers *by Tad Crawford and Eva Doman Bruck* (208 pages, 8½" X 11", $19.95)

Business and Legal Forms for Illustrators *by Tad Crawford* (160 pages, 8⅞" X 11", $15.95)

Business and Legal Forms for Photographers *by Tad Crawford* (192 pages, 8½" X 11", $18.95)

Legal Guide for the Visual Artist *by Tad Crawford* (224 pages, 7" X 12", $18.95)

How to Sell Your Photographs and Illustrations *by Elliott and Barbara Gordon* (128 pages, 8" X 10", $16.95)

The Business of Being an Artist *by Dan Grant* (224 pages, 6" X 9", $16.95)

The Family Legal Companion *by Thomas Hauser* (256 pages, 6" X 9", $16.95)

How to Shoot Stock Photos that Sell *by Michal Heron* (192 pages, 8" X 10", $16.95)

Stock Photo Forms *by Michal Heron* (32 pages, 8½" X 11", $8.95)

The Photographer's Assistant *by John Kieffer* (208 pages, 6¾" X 10", $16.95)

Travel Photography: A Complete Guide to How to Shoot and Sell *by Susan McCartney* (384 pages,6¾" X 10", $22.95)

The Graphic Designer's Basic Guide to the Macintosh *by Michael Meyerowitz and Sam Sanchez* (144 pages, 8" X 10", $19.95)

Hers: The Wise Woman's Guide to Starting a Business on $2,000 or Less *by Carol Milano* (208 pages, 6" X 9", $12.95)

The Artist's Complete Health and Safety Guide *by Monona Rossol* (328 pages, 6" X 9", $16.95)

Stage Fright *by Monona Rossol* (144 pages, 6" X 9", $12.95)

Electronic Design and Publishing: Business Practices by Liane Sebastian (112 pages, 6¾" X 10", $19.95)

Overexposure: Health Hazards in Photography *by Susan Shaw and Monona Rossol* (320 pages, 6¾" X 10", $18.95)

Caring for Your Art *by Jill Snyder* (176 pages, 6" X 9", $14.95)

Please write to request our free catalog. If you wish to order a book, send your check or money order to:
Allworth Press, 10 East 23rd Street, Suite 400, New York, New York 10010.
To pay for shipping and handling, include $3 for the first book ordered and $1 for each additional book ($7 plus $1 if the order is from Canada). New York State residents must add sales tax.